All the Best
Jim Webb

9-24-2016

Otsego Creative arts
Festival

The Tractor

Steven Wilkens

Other Steven Wilkens Titles

The Long Hot Summer

Tattooed Angels

Nana's Willow

Redemption

The Lost Tribe

The Sword of David

Transport

The Passage

Harvest Moon

Coincidental Journey

Essence of Courage

Happy Oscar (the Model A)

Having My Say

This Book is dedicated to

George Galloway

And

David Kidder

Two men that exemplify

Generosity and a kind spirit for
helping others.

A heart-felt thanks to some very special people that went out of their way to assist me in making this book as good as I could make it.

First and foremost: Miss Becky, she's always in my corner and my biggest supporter

Helen Kidder, who went way beyond anything I had hoped for. Her insight was incredible.

To Rick and Marcie Bonney, Kathy Pasch, and Marge Abbott for all their help in editing and proof reading

The Tractor

1

John Liggett stepped into the kitchen of his small three bedroom home and flipped on the overhead light. It would be another couple of hours before the sun would make an appearance. He was an early riser, and had been so since growing up on a family farm. At this moment everything seemed as it always had, he would get up somewhere between 3 and 4am. While Janice, or Jan as she liked to be called, would sleep in until 7 or 8.

He pressed the button on the coffee maker to get it started while he went to the bathroom to shower and shave. When he returned to the kitchen the coffee was made. He truly loved his first cup of coffee in the morning. He would enjoy the rich aroma and flavor while he sat at the table and started putting together his daily to-do list. This morning, he had to smile, he truly was a creature of habit.

He had retired from his job as a senior retail executive a few years back, and yet the only change to his morning ritual was not going to work. Since his retirement, he had taken to writing a family history that he planned on handing down to his two daughters when it was finished. He would sit at the table with his tablet and a spiral notebook and work on research until Jan finally woke up and made her morning appearance. Jan was a hard sleeper and when she finally stepped into the kitchen her hair was a tangled mess and her face bore the red lines caused by creases in the pillow. Their morning rituals were consistent. He would say, "Good morning, beautiful." To which she always replied, "You really do need to make an eye doctor appointment." Then she would proceed to get herself some coffee, which by this time, the pot held barely half a cup.

Sometimes she would comment that it would be nice if she could start her day with a whole cup of coffee, but usually, she just took a sip and quickly made another pot while John got up and made a couple of bagels, one for her with butter and honey, one with cream cheese and jam for himself.

They would eat and chat a bit, then she was off to the bathroom for her shower and makeup. An hour later she would emerge. A strikingly beautiful transition had taken place and John always made some lame come-on comment that made her laugh. Then she was off to work as a retail clerk at a very busy pharmacy. She had worked there for over twenty-five years and John never could figure out why. Every day was the same, she was driven crazy by hundreds of people that would come in and expect her to know their names, their spouse's names and the names of their children. While they themselves rarely knew what kind of insurance they had, let alone what their co-pay was. The recent changes in the laws regarding security and privacy compounded the problems. In all fairness, many of the people were not feeling well and had just spent an hour waiting to see their doctor. Then the doctor told them that he was prescribing a certain medicine for them and that they could go get it at the pharmacy. Problem being, the customer had been waiting at the pharmacy for another hour and the doctor's office had yet to fax over the prescription. For all of this, the customer placed the blame squarely on Jan's shoulders.

Every night she would come home exhausted and stressed out. John had suggested that she quit and find something else to do, but for whatever reason, she refused to do so. Maybe it had to do with familiarity, or that she only had a few more years until her own retirement, but she was determined to tough it out.

This morning John sat at the table thinking these thoughts and half expecting Jan to shuffle into the kitchen at any moment. In fact, he yearned for that to happen. It wasn't going to, he knew that, but still he wanted it so badly it hurt. It had been just three weeks since Jan had passed away in her sleep from a cerebral aneurism. He hadn't even noticed that she was gone. He had gotten up, made the coffee, showered and started working on the family history. It wasn't until long past the time she usually got up that he noticed she hadn't joined him and that if she didn't get up now, she would have to rush getting ready and she hated that. He went upstairs to wake her and was stunned to find her lifeless body, already cold to the touch.

He had called 911 first, and then their daughters. The next several hours went by in a blur. First the police and paramedics, who were nothing but kind and professional. Then came the crying and hugging with his daughters and their families. It took several hours for Wendy to get there. John doesn't remember crying himself, maybe he did, but he didn't remember it. He just played the role he had always played, the strong one everyone could lean on, and the girls needed that. Then there was the autopsy to deal with. His poor, beautiful Janice was being dissected just so he and his family could have the knowledge of why she died so suddenly. While that was going on, there were funeral arrangements to be made, a casket to be selected, cemetery plots to be bought, an obituary to write, a dress and jewelry to be chosen for her burial, pallbearers to be selected, and family and friends to call, the worst of which was the call to Jan's elderly parents. The strangest call of all was to Jan's employer. Not once did he offer any condolences, instead he just kept mumbling about what he had to do to cover the sales counter that morning. After a couple of minutes of listening to such nonsense, John finally just told him to find another housewife that would enslave herself for ten bucks an hour and hung up.

The funeral was almost surreal. So many people showed up at the funeral home, that a line of people formed waiting to get in. John and his daughters and their families were in a state of shock and mechanically greeted everyone and listened to their stories of how they knew Jan, and what she had meant to them. Many of the stories were heart-wrenching. John was amazed at what his quiet, unassuming wife had meant to so many. Some, mostly customers at the pharmacy, told of how she had patiently helped them, often with a smile and a kind word. Some even handed John a few dollars, telling him that when they had picked up a prescription, they hadn't expected it to be so much and found themselves short on funds and that Jan had paid the difference out of her pocket. Just during the visitation more than a dozen, such people handed him money, making him wonder how many more she had helped that he would never know about.

He didn't remember much about the funeral itself. A number of people got up and spoke about what a kind and loving woman Jan had been, or what a great friend. During it all, John was lost in his own thoughts and memories. Then the trip out to the cemetery. The long line of cars, the beautiful warm, sunny day, and watching the six pallbearers: their son-in-law, Jason, Grandson Grant, a co-worker of hers, and three neighbors, lift the dark green casket, (her favorite color), from the hearse and carry it to the grave. As he sat there on the row of chairs before the casket, John didn't hear much of what the preacher was saying. He was just longing to feel her touch once more.

Then as if a sign from God, a beautiful butterfly landed on his knee. He felt like it was the spirit of Jan telling him that everything was going to be okay.

After the funeral came the big lunch, which was nice. John had always thought the idea of having a big lunch after burying someone was a dumb custom, but now he understood it. It provided the first step in getting on with life. The first step in the healing process. It provided an opportunity for friends and neighbors to reconnect with others they hadn't seen in a long time. It also was a time for close friends and family to offer their support and any help that John might need, which at the time he had no clue what that might be. He would soon learn that while a talented manager, he lacked plenty of basic survival skills such as cooking a decent meal for himself.

He didn't have to worry about that for the first three days after Jan's funeral. Daughter Wendy and her family lived out of state, so just the girls and she had come home for the funeral and stayed with him. Wendy was a great cook, just like her mother had been, but friends and neighbors had brought over so much food that if Wendy and the girls hadn't been there, most of it would have spoiled. In truth, Wendy and the girls being there had been a gift from God. He didn't have time to feel sorry for himself, as those little girls brightened each moment and made him grateful for their time together. The older two daughters understood the situation, but almost every day the youngest would go upstairs looking for Grammy, and then cry when told Grammy wasn't here.

John and Jan's marriage had produced two beautiful and loving daughters, Debbie, the oldest, and Wendy, their baby. John and Jan had always been very proud of the women their daughters had become. They had enjoyed a close, loving relationship with them. The girls depended on their father for help with life's big issues, but it was their mother that got daily calls about the day to day issues. It was probably because of this habit of calling their mother every day that both girls continued to call him and check on how he was doing. Jan's friends, their extended family, the neighbors, and even people he hadn't talked to in years, all called and checked on him. All offered their condolences and offered what help they could. He knew they meant the very best, but he was sure that the next person to ask him how he was doing would get a reply like; "How would I know? No one has given me the time to figure that out!"

So here he sat, sipping his morning coffee, watching the morning news and thinking about making a bagel. He hadn't done that since the morning before Jan died. What made this morning different was that he was actually considering the future. A future without Jan, his future. True to the way John thought of things, he realized that whether that future would be good or bad was entirely up to him. He was sad that Jan was gone, but he wasn't mad at God for taking her. Instead, he gave thanks for the 40 plus years God had granted them together.

As he took inventory of his feelings and options, he got up from the table, stepped over to the refrigerator, retrieved a bagel and popped it into the toaster. While the smell of baking bread filled his senses, he reached for the top right drawer and pulled his notebook from it. It was time to start making to-do lists again. When the bagel popped up in the toaster, he reached back into the refrigerator for the cream cheese and then paused a moment before grabbing the tub of butter instead, and then the bottle of honey from the cupboard. After making the bagel, he refilled his coffee and sat down to start on his list.

2

As was usual while working on his to-do list, he thought about what he felt like doing. That thought made him frown. What he felt like doing was hold his wife, the love of his life, in his arms and tell her how beautiful she was and how much he loved her. Those thoughts, he realized, were so unproductive. They only made him miss her all the more. And he missed her so much that it hurt physically. Every time he heard the house creak, he imagined her walking around as she used to do. Maybe she was still here; he just couldn't see her. He knew she was in heaven, but thinking of her being close helped.

He tried to find something that would take all day to do, and that would occupy his mind. He wanted a bigger task and something he could break down into smaller bits. It was how he had always done his lists. Suddenly, an image from a month ago, of Jan standing next to the sink popped into his mind. She had told him that he needed to clean out the garage. She had hit a couple of boxes the night before pulling into the garage when she had returned from work. He decided that the garage was what he would tackle that day.

Having decided what to do, now he pondered how to do it. He figured that he would break the big job down into a number of little jobs, but how best to do that? Number one on the list was to move his truck and Jan's car out of the garage. Number two was to move ten boxes to the center of the garage floor and sort through them. He figured there would be four types of things he would be sorting. Things that should have been thrown out long ago, Jan's things that he would let the girls sort through and take what they wanted, his things that he still wanted, and finally the things he no longer wanted.

He had just finished the list and refilled his coffee cup when his oldest daughter, Debbie, called to see if he was doing okay. He told her he was, and she acted like she didn't believe him and asked if he had eaten something. He assured her that he had and that he was fine, and then he told her about his plan to clean the garage. She thought that was a grand idea and suggested that he should hold a garage sale.

"Geez, I don't know about that," John started to argue. "Not sure I want people picking through our stuff."

"Oh, come on Dad, it'll be fun. Maybe Wendy can come home for it." Debbie argued.

From the moment he walked into the garage, he realized what a monumental task he had before him. It only looked slightly more manageable with the vehicles out of the way. He figured he would start with the left side of the garage and work that half all the way to the back wall. As he had written down on his list, he grabbed ten boxes and pulled them to the center of the floor and opened the first one. Half of those boxes were filled with old clothes, half his and half Jan's. He sat Jan's clothes off to the side and boxed his up for donation or for the garage sale, should he decide to have one. Deep down, he knew he would. Debbie suggested it, which meant she wanted to have it, and his one weakness was his inability to say no to either of his girls. He smiled at the memory of when Grant, Debbie's oldest son, had been born. He was thrilled to have a grandson, but he remembered thinking "great a boy!" Maybe now there was someone in this family I will be able to say "no" to."

By noon, he had made it halfway down the left side of the garage. Surprisingly, he had found a number of boxes filled with things they had saved that should have been thrown out years ago. The more of those things he found, the more he realized that the value he put on things had changed, and probably very recently.

He had just pulled the next ten boxes to the center of the garage when his cell phone went off.

"Hi Dad," it was Wendy. "I hear you're having a garage sale."

"I heard that too," John smiled.

"Are you sure that you're ready for that?"

"Yes, I think so," John replied honestly. "Your Mom had asked me to clean out the garage about a month ago, and the only way to do that is either sell the stuff or donate it."

"I suppose you're right," Wendy said. "Maybe doing it now will help you get on with things. I talked to Debbie a few minutes ago."

"I figured as much."

Wendy laughed. "Anyway, I like the idea of coming home to help out, if we can afford it."

"I'll buy the plane tickets, you just book them."

"Great, thanks, Daddy. When?"

"How about the weekend after next?"

"Okay, great. I'll book the flight for me and the girls. We'll come in on Wednesday so we can help you set up."

"That would be great," John replied. "Here is my card information…"

By the time Wendy's flight arrived, John had gone through every box and had already disposed of the items he felt were not worthy of a good garage sale. He had also rounded up enough tables for everything to be placed upon and several racks for hanging clothes and such. He then set up benches to display tools he no longer needed or wanted and had gone through the house in search of more. All in all, it took Debbie and Wendy the entire day on Wednesday to get everything marked at a price that would ensure sales. And surprisingly, they took little of their mother's things for themselves. Wendy couldn't take much because she would have to either carry it on the plane or box it up and ship it home. Debbie probably took little to keep Wendy from feeling bad.

Thursday morning at the crack of dawn, Wendy was up and making breakfast for her girls and Dad. An hour later Debbie arrived with her two sons, Grant, and J.J. (Jason Jr.). Debbie had had two long term relationships before marrying Jason Sr. The first was with Grant's father, and everything seemed good until Grant was born and his father decided that he didn't really like to work. Debbie held on for another year, but finally, just couldn't afford to raise two boys. The second relationship lasted ten years. This fellow was a hard worker but had a mean and indifferent side to him that he showed only to her. When she could take no more of it, she came home. Jason Sr. was a young man that John worked with, and he introduced them and they hit it off right away and she finally found happiness.

J.J. was almost two and a terror to keep up with. Luckily, he loved Wendy's girls and they felt the same about him and did a wonderful job of keeping him occupied. Grant, on the other hand, was fifteen, very tall and slim. He was strikingly handsome but quiet and shy. At school, he put in an appearance and little else, and he didn't seem to be interested in much of anything except video games and girls. John and Jan occasionally had him over to spend the day and night at their house on weekends. Even hired him to help with certain tasks around the house, none of which he took much interest in.

Grant was growing up; however, and John could see it in him. He was still a bit lethargic, but when asked to help with something, he stepped right up and did a good job of it. John and Grant moved all the tables out along the driveway and carried the bigger items out. On one of the trips to and from the garage, Grant noticed the old family tractor sitting in the back corner of the garage.

"Are you going to bring that old tractor out?"

"No," was John's quick and firm reply.

"I didn't even know you had a tractor," Grant said. "Have you always had it?"

"Ever since my dad died," John replied. "Your great grandfather bought that tractor brand new in 1953. It was the first motorized vehicle he ever owned. Used it for years until it was just too worn out. Then he parked it in the barn and there it sat until he gave it to me just before he passed away."

12

"What are you going to do with it?"

"Always thought I would restore it one day," John smiled as he picked up one end of a table and motioned for Grant to grab the other end.

"That would be cool," Grant said as he took the other end of the table. "But then what? What would you do with a tractor here in town?"

John laughed, "I'd probably drive it around."

"Really?" Grant seemed to like that idea.

"Maybe even get a trailer to haul it behind my pickup, go to shows and the county fair."

"That would be fun," Grant said as they walked back to the garage for the next table.

3

The garage sale was an experience for John. He had never seen so many different types of people, all with the one thread of character that united them; the search for a bargain. He had told the girls when they were pricing things to mark them cheap. If the stuff didn't sell, it was getting donated, so whatever they got for something was better than nothing. Also, if it sold, the buyer would take it away and he wouldn't have to haul it away himself. Even with ridiculously cheap prices, people haggled. He left the girls to handle the haggling, and he realized an hour into the sale that it had been the right decision. For his stuff, he would have accepted any offer. Jan's things, however, he thought they were giving them away. When one of Jan's favorite dresses caught a woman's eye, and she offered a dollar instead of the five it was marked, he almost stepped in to take it from her hand. Luckily, Wendy was there and negotiated an agreeable price of three dollars.

Grant wandered around like he was lost. He was on hand to help customers load things, and did so without a complaint unless it was his mother that asked. Twice John thought of saying something to the boy, but in the back of his mind, he heard Jan telling him to stay out of it unless they asked for his advice. When not helping load something, Grant would walk around the tables and look things over or go into the garage and look the tractor over, twice getting up in the seat and holding the steering wheel in his hands.

In some respects, the sale was the funeral all over again. Dozens of people that came had been friends, neighbors, and co-workers of either Jan's or his. All wanted to talk about Jan, offer condolences and wish him well. A dozen different fellows asked about the tractor. Two made good offers even after being told it wasn't for sale.

Around noon, John took Grant with him to get food for everyone and when they got back they had to park a block away and carry the food back. As they handed the food out, John noticed that Grant had gone over to help a couple of young female customers. They were looking through Jan's clothes and were particularly interested in things she saved but hadn't worn in decades. When one of the girls took a pantsuit off the hanger and held it in front of herself, John had to smile. It was the outfit Jan had worn on their first date back in the late 70's, and Grant was right there complimenting the girl on how she would look in it. The boy was a good salesman, the girl bought the outfit without haggling.

About the time those girls had left with their new treasures and Debbie had gotten Grant to sit down and eat something, another family came up the drive with two teenage daughters. John noticed this family for several reasons. First, they reminded him of his own family when he was their age. They had two daughters with about the same age spread as Wendy and Debbie. Also, the family were good looking people. The man with rugged but handsome features. The wife with a petite frame and pretty face without a trace of makeup. The two daughters were even more beautiful than their mother, having just the right touch of their father's genes in them. The thing that really stood out, however, was the evidence that they were less than affluent. Their clothes were old and well-worn, and John had noticed that they were driving an old rusted out car that belched blue smoke from the exhaust pipe.

Watching them get out, he noticed that both girls had to get out of the right rear door.

The woman and both daughters wore glasses that had been repaired with tape. The family was quiet and pretty much clung together until the father started looking at the tools and the women moved over to Jan's clothes. Watching the women go through the clothes, John realized that they were hanging items they liked together so they could easily compare them later after they had looked through everything. As they sorted through the clothes, the three women spoke to each other in hushed whispers, but he was able to catch enough words to realize that the girls had been told that they would only be able to select one item each and it couldn't be more than a dollar.

The man seemed to be looking for a particular tool, and when he didn't seem to find it, he slowly turned away from the table.

"Looking for something special?" John asked as he stepped up to the tool table.

"Yes," the man nodded. "I was hoping to find a 9/16 flex socket."

"I don't have extras of that," John explained. "These are all the duplicates I have that I felt I wouldn't be needing. Just filling out your collection or have a special job in mind?"

"I have to replace the radiator in my car and the way they build things nowadays, you can't get at them easily. I would just go buy a new one, but with the price of a new radiator, even from the salvage yard, I can't afford a new socket as well."

"I hear you," John agreed. "You from around here?"

"Yeah, just across town." The man answered.

"Tell you what," John found himself feeling sorry for the fellow. "If you bring it back when you're done, I'll loan you my flex socket."

"You would do that for me, a stranger?"

"Well, yeah. I want it back of course." John replied.

"Oh of course," the man nodded his head. "I promise to bring it back as soon as I am done."

"Okay then, let's go get it." John turned and motioned toward the garage.

Grant was eating his hamburger when he noticed the three women going through the clothes. He wasn't one to miss an opportunity, so he sat his burger down and went over to see if he could help them. The girls just smiled and stepped back shyly. The mother smiled and shook her head. "We're just looking, thank you."

"Okay," Grant felt awkward. "If you need anything, just ask."

"Thank you, we will."

As soon as John and the father entered the garage, the man noticed the old Ford tractor back in the corner. "A 1953 Jubilee!" He said with a smile.

John turned and looked at the man. "You can tell that from there?"

"Of course," the man laughed. "The nose badge gives it away. If that badge was missing, the best I could do would be to tell you that it was either a Jubilee or an NAA. But if I could look at the hydraulic pump I would know for certain."

"Really?" John was impressed.

"Yes, the Jubilee had a Vickers vane pump which was square. While the NAA which is just like the 1953 Jubilee, but built in 1954, had a piston pump which is round. The 1953 Jubilee model had the special nose badge in honor of Ford Motor Company's 50th anniversary."

"Couldn't someone have swapped out the nose badges?" John asked.

"Oh sure, and just about every other part on them," the man laughed. "But for all practical purposes, people call either the Jubilee or the NAA a 'Jubie'."

"How do you know so much about old tractors?" John asked.

"Was born and raised on a farm," The man replied.

"Why did you come to town?"

"We lost the farm and everything we had worked for," the man frowned.

"I am sorry," John really meant that.

"Thank you, I am too."

The women had finally settled on an outfit for each of them and brought the clothes up to the table for Debbie to collect for. One of the girls had been sneaking glances at Grant ever since he had offered help. Twice he caught her looking his way, but each time she quickly looked away. Now as they stepped close to where he was, he smiled at the girl and she shyly smiled back and then turned her eyes toward the ground.

Suddenly Grant felt like he knew her, or, at least had seen her before. "Do you attend Fillmore?"

She didn't openly reply, just nodded her head.

"I do too," Grant offered.

"I know," She replied with a smile that revealed a mouth with numerous chipped or broken teeth. "I've seen you there."

By this time the father had come out of the garage, the mother had settled her account, and the girls were turning to go.

"Maybe I'll see you on Monday," Grant offered as the last comment. Exactly why, he didn't have a clue, but the girl kind of intrigued him.

She turned and smiled. "Maybe." Then she turned and walked away with her family.

"They find some clothes?" John asked of Debbie.

"Each of them got one outfit for a dollar," Debbie replied. "Didn't even haggle, paid me in quarters."

"Quarters?"

"Twelve quarters," Debbie confirmed.

"I see," John said and then turned toward Grant. "Do you know the girl?"

"Not really," Grant shrugged. "Just seen her at school."

"Ah," John nodded. "Well, whatever doesn't sell, we are going to give to them, if they'll accept them."

"Why wouldn't they accept them?" Grant asked. "Gram's clothes are far better than what they have now."

"Maybe, but maybe they bought those clothes with money they had earned."

"So?" Grant didn't get it.

"Pride, son. Pride." John replied.

4

The garage sale went far better than John would have guessed. A lot of Jan's clothes sold, along with all of his extra tools and almost all of the stuff he called junk. The sale had brought in nearly a thousand dollars. He gave a hundred to Grant for helping, and divided the rest between Debbie and Wendy. All three of them tried to turn his offer down, but the way John saw it, he was just going to donate all that stuff anyway. It was the girls that put the sale together and got everything marked at a price that it would actually sell at.

The sale was also a great idea as it brought out old friends and neighbors, as well as gave John almost an entire week to enjoy his granddaughters. He was, however, glad that it was over. What had been a cramped garage was now neat and orderly, with the exception of the remaining dozen or so boxes of things to be donated or disposed of in some fashion.

On Monday, he took Wendy and the girls to the airport and on the way home thought of ways to spend his time. Life at this stage was not what he had planned for, but with the exception of losing Jan, he had no complaints. Since he was now alone, and not anchored to the house because of Jan still working, he thought he might take off right after Christmas and travel around the deep south for the balance of the winter. Debbie or Grant could check in on the house once a week or so, leaving him to follow the sunshine.

On Tuesday, he spent the day sorting through the items that hadn't sold at the sale and decided which items he would just throw out with his trash. As he was sorting through the stuff, the fellow that had borrowed the tools pulled into the drive. As John watched him get out of his old car, an idea formed quickly in his mind.

"Get the new radiator installed?" John asked with a smile and an extended hand.

"Well, not a new one," the man took John's hand. "Found a cheap used one in a local salvage yard."

"Sometimes, they're not much better than what you are taking out," John cautioned.

"Well, it doesn't leak," the man replied. "Let's hope it lasts a while. I wanted to get these tools back to you as soon as I could."

"I appreciate that," John smiled and took the tools the man was handing over. He stepped over to the tool box and put the tools back where they belonged.

"Looks like you had a successful sale," the man commented.

"Indeed," John nodded toward the dozen boxes containing the remainder of what didn't sell. It was time to put his plan into action. "Now comes the hardest part of all for me."

"What's that?"

John looked the man in the eye and smiled a sad smile. "I was married for 40 years to a beautiful girl that I loved with all my heart. She always had a way of looking like she spent a lot of money on her clothes, but was actually a very thrifty shopper."

The man just nodded his understanding.

"Now I have to load all those clothes up and go dump them off at some charitable organization and who knows who will end up with them. I would be much more comfortable, and I know Jan would be pleased if I could give them to someone personally. Someone, I know that would appreciate them as she did."

When the man didn't say anything, just nodded his head in agreement, John had to go a bit farther than he had planned. "Say, your wife and daughters are close to Jan's size. Would you do me a huge favor?"

"Like what?"

"Take those boxes over there," John pointed at the seven or eight boxes holding Jan's clothes. "Let your women go through them and take as much as they want, then just donate the rest."

The man just looked at him without committing.

"It would mean a great deal to me." John told him.

"Why?"

"Because I know it would please my late wife to know that her clothes, that she took such care in selecting, would be going to women like her that would appreciate them as she did."

"It would mean that much to you?" The man asked.

"It would," John replied.

"I know they loved the clothes when we were at your sale, it was hard for them to choose."

"Then you would be doing everyone a favor," John smiled. "Not to mention saving me the pain of having to take Jan's clothes to Goodwill."

The man looked up at John and smiled. "Okay, let's load them up. The girls will be thrilled."

They loaded the boxes into the car and the man shook John's hand and thanked him. After the man had left, John felt pretty good about how everything had worked out. He closed up the garage and made his way into the house. He paused a moment in front of an 8x10 photograph of Jan and himself. It was the last one to be taken of them. He reached out and touched the picture, his heart heavy. He missed her so much right now it physically hurt.

5

He rubbed the spot on her cheek in the picture. In his mind he could almost feel her soft skin, hear her laugh, see her rolling her eyes at his antics. He dropped his hand to his side and stepped back from the picture. He had to get his emotions under control. He deeply loved her and missed her greatly, but knew she was in heaven with Jesus, and one day he would see her again. Suddenly, the door chime rang and snapped him out of his self-pity. He wasn't sure if that was a good thing, but it was what it was.

He went to the front door and opened it to find a good looking woman of about his age, holding a couple of covered dishes. She was dressed in a snug sweater dress of dark gray with black stripes across the breast line, with dark leggings and shiny black heels. She had beautiful red hair, but not the color one might expect for a woman her age, so he decided it was probably colored. Her green eyes, however, put that decision in doubt. She wore stylish wire frame glasses and a touch more makeup than Jan would have used. All of this had taken John's mind less than three seconds to take in and file away. Less time in fact than it took the woman to speak.

She spoke in a high pitched tone of voice that instantly made John think that maybe the next time she went shopping she should consider buying the next size larger panties.

"John, I was so sorry to hear of Janice's passing." The woman started. John had no idea who this woman was. "She was such a saint and such a remarkable gardener. I just loved her flowers."

John just nodded his head.

25

WAS HE EVER A SAILOR.

"I didn't want to bother you right after the funeral. I know how that can be. I lost my husband Bill four years ago last April. And for the first two weeks after that, I talked to and hugged more people than I have during the rest of my life."

"You're right about that," John smiled.

"And they brought so much food that half of it went to waste."

Again John nodded his agreement.

"However, since it has been a few weeks now," the woman sure could rattle on quickly. "I don't know how well you are in the kitchen, but my Bill was lucky if he could find the stove, let alone make something on it."

That made John laugh.

"I hope you don't mind, but I put together a little something for you. If you do cook, well, you won't have to tonight. If you don't cook, then at least, you can have a good supper tonight." She held the dishes out for him to take.

"That's very gracious of you..."

"Stephanie, Stephanie Carson," The woman replied. "From just down the street. I know we've never met, but I knew Janice quite well."

"Well, please," John said and motioned for her to come in. "Would you like a cup of coffee?"

"Why, that's very neighborly of you. Yes, I would love some." She replied while quickly stepping through the open door.

John led her into the kitchen and she perched herself on a barstool at the counter while he pulled a cup from the cupboard and filled it with coffee that was hours old. "This coffee isn't the freshest. If it is too strong, I'll make some fresh." He offered as he handed her the cup.

"I love my coffee, hot, strong and straight," Stephanie smiled.

They talked for over an hour and through another entire pot of coffee. John was having a hard time reading why she was there exactly. Just being neighborly, or sending him some kind of signal? She went on and on about the neighborhood and all the crazy people that live in it. John was wishing he had simply thanked her for the food and left it at that. Finally, as she was leaving, John asked her where he could return the dishes. She seemed surprised that he didn't already know.

"I live just four houses down," she motioned the direction with her finger.

"I am terribly sorry," John explained. "I'm the type of person that tends to get lost in my own little world and not pay much attention to what is going on around me. Jan was the social one."

Stephanie smiled and reached out and touched his arm. "That's all right. Not being nosey is nothing to apologize for. If you need anything, anything at all, just ask, okay?"

"I'll do that," John smiled and walked her to the door. "And thanks again."

By the time she did finally leave, it was after 3 and John knew Debbie would be getting off work before long.

He realized that Stephanie had brought over more food than he could eat alone, and it gave him a perfect cover for having Debbie over for the real reason he needed to see her tonight. That reason was for advice on how to handle situations such as what had just happened. He meant to call her at work but dialed the home phone by mistake. After the second ring, Grant answered.

"Grant?"

"Hi Papa."

"What are you doing at your Mom's workplace?"

"You dialed the house number, Papa." Grant replied.

"Okay, then what are you doing at home and not in school?"

"I got a three-day holiday."

"I see," John said, knowing there was more to it but didn't want to get into that at the moment. "I am calling to ask you, J.J., and your mother over for dinner tonight."

"Thank you Papa, but I am going to my Dad's for the rest of the week."

"You're going to miss a great meal. A neighbor brought over lasagna, bread rolls, and a great looking tossed salad."

"Sounds great," Grant replied. "But it is probably best if I stay out of Mom's sight for now."

"Something you need to talk about?" John asked.

"No, but thanks anyway."

28

"Okay, but if you change your mind, call me."

"I will Papa, thanks."

Just a little after 6 Debbie, Jason and J.J. arrived for dinner. Jason explained that he had been given the night off because of business being slow. John asked Debbie to heat the lasagna up while he got the plates and utensils out. While they prepared for dinner, John told her about Stephanie's visit. Debbie was laughing by the time he finished the story.

"What do you find so funny?"

"Oh my word, Dad!" Debbie laughed. "You have a suitor and don't even know it."

"I just buried my wife," John protested. "If she was doing what you think she was, that is wrong on so many levels."

"Maybe," Debbie nodded as she took the lasagna out of the microwave. "On the other hand, she said she knew Mom, and may have admired you from afar."

"She called your mother Janice." John pointed out.

"Yeah, so?"

"If she had really known your mother as well as she was letting on, she would have called her Jan. No one that knew her well called her Janice, not even her own parents."

"Okay, you may have a point," Debbie conceded. "Just remember that 'close' is objective. What's close for you and me, may not be the same for her. Also, remember some people are not meant to live alone. I know people that

29

have lost a spouse and have remarried within months. It's not that they didn't dearly love their deceased spouse, it is simply a matter of not being able to function alone. She told you that her husband had died several years ago. So, if she is someone that can't stand being alone, she might have seen an opportunity and simply couldn't resist taking the chance. You know, get you before some other lucky widow does."

John looked at his daughter a moment and just shook his head.

"Well?" Debbie laughed.

"Did I ever tell you how smart I think you are?"

"And beautiful too, huh?"

John laughed. "Smart and beautiful, a very dangerous combination."

"You got that right," Jason agreed.

Over dinner, the topic of discussion was Grant and what was going on with him. He appeared to have lost interest in all the things Debbie thought were important. "He was never good in school, but this year it appears that he had just given up. He doesn't do his homework, he doesn't participate in class.

Debbie explained, "His teachers say he attends the class physically, but they have no clue where his mind is at."

"Do you think he is into drugs?" John asked

"At first I did, but we have searched his room, several times," Debbie answered.

"Each time we have come up dry," Jason added. "In fact, we found nothing other than one would expect to find in a teenage boy's room. I even did a little snooping around about his friends. Talked to teachers and others. He doesn't hang with bad kids."

"How is he when not in school?" John asked.

"Typical teenager," Debbie replied. "Good most of the time just wants to be left alone mostly. Does like playing with J.J. though. Other times he seems irritated."

"Bored, most likely," Jason offered. "We have a little house, with a little yard. He is a big boy, probably feels a bit cooped up."

"Possibly," John agreed. "What was he expelled for?"

"Threatening another student with violence." Jason answered.

"Fighting?" John asked to be sure. The way people talked now days was just crazy.

"Not even fighting," Debbie replied. "Just threatening it."

"Good Lord in Heaven," John sighed. "In my day, the teachers would have stood back and let us work it out; then sent us to the restroom to wash up and get back to class."

"Things are different now, Dad."

6

The following morning, John decided that he wasn't ready to deal with Stephanie just yet. Deep down he also knew that the longer he delayed, the more complex the meeting might be. However, if he returned the dishes too soon, it might look like he was eager to see her again. "Oh dear Lord in heaven," John thought to himself. "I thought this kind of thing was well in my past." He decided that what he needed was to keep himself busy, so he started with mowing the yard and doing something with Jan's beautiful gardens.

Mowing the yard was simple and straight forward. He had done it thousands of times, but the gardens were another matter entirely. Jan had been so gifted in so many areas. She was crafty, creative, and had a remarkable sense of style. She could make things in a matter of minutes that simply blew people away. The gardens were just an extension of that talent. They were balanced. A tasteful mix of just the right plants to give the viewer pleasure. A blend of colors and textures gave the eye something new to find at every glance.

Now John stood there with the garden hose in his hand and sprinkling those beautiful flowers. He suddenly realized that he had no clue what type of flowers 90% of them were. Then he realized that not all of the plants would require the same amount of water. He quickly shut the hose off, wondering if he might have already drowned some of Jan's precious plants. He realized that if he was to properly take care of these plants, he better find a way to learn how. Maybe Debbie would know something about that although she had never shown any tenacities in that area.

Saturday morning John decided to go out for breakfast. On the way to his favorite restaurant, he passed a small marina with a dozen pontoon boats parked out front with big sale banners attached to them. He instantly thought about stopping by after breakfast to check them out. It would give him something to do, and if he found one he liked and could afford, he would have something to do all summer, fish.

After breakfast, he stopped by the bank and then drove over to the marina and started walking around the boats. Within minutes, a heavy-set middle-aged man in a bright blue polo shirt sporting the marina's logo and a pair of khaki slacks walked up to the boat John was looking at.

"Looking for a boat?" The man asked with a big smile.

"I don't know," John shrugged. "Just driving by and noticed the sale banners. Thought I would have a look."

"If you find one you like, how do you plan on using it?" The man asked.

"I thought maybe putting it in water," John replied, thinking it was a stupid question.

The man roared with laughter. "Oh, that's a good one! This is what I meant, however. If you had a pontoon boat, would you use it for just trolling along looking at scenery, or have family and friends aboard for a mobile party? Use it for fishing maybe, or multi-functions? Such as all the fore-mentioned plus water-skiing. How you plan on using it makes a difference in which one will fill those needs."

John turned and looked at the man. "That's the best darn sales pitch I have ever heard."

Again the man laughed. "I don't see my job as selling, say this boat here." The man laid his hand on the first boat in the line. "My job is not selling boats at all. Instead, my job is that of a consultant, helping people find the right fit in a boat."

John thought about that for a moment. "What I think I will use it for," John began. "My wife and I always loved the river and used to rent canoes and spend an afternoon just paddling and taking in the beauty."

"So just trolling?" The man asked. "Your wife still like doing that?"

"She passed," John quietly replied.

"I am truly sorry," The man offered. "Recently?"

"A month ago."

"Very recently," The man replied. "I am sorry. Are you thinking about a boat as a way to occupy time?"

"Yes," John answered honestly.

"Have you given it much thought?"

"Not really, just saw the banners and thought I'd check it out, why?"

"Well," the man began. "If you truly want a boat, I'll help you find one. If, however, you are just looking for something to take the pain of loss away, you might be disappointed in owning a boat."

"Why?"

"One of the biggest and best parts of owning a boat and spending time on the water is that it gives one a chance to relax. Time to chill and also time to think. It is that thinking that may be helpful or maybe not."

"Very insightful of you, thank you," John smiled at the man. "What I was thinking was that I would like one that would be good for fishing on the river, maybe taking the family and having a picnic, and having enough power to pull a tube might be nice too. Have a teenage grandson. He would probably enjoy a little tubing."

The man asked more questions, and then with an air of professionalism, showed several boats to John and covered each of the boat's pros and cons. Finally, they settled on a red and white one that offered everything John thought he was looking for. The problem was that at $20,000.00 it was far more than John had planned on spending on a boat. Part of that was for a lot more luxury features than John had expected. When the price negotiations started, the man asked him if he had anything he could trade in? The only thing that came to his mind was Jan's car, and because it was an older model, the man couldn't afford to give him much for it.

John decided that he wouldn't trade the car in. He wasn't sure he was ready to get rid of it yet anyway. He was convinced that he wanted the boat, so he put five grand down and financed the balance for 12 months. He knew he had a certificate of deposit maturing in a couple of months that would cover the rest of the boat's cost. Then the salesman made sure John's truck was setup to tow the boat. When that was checked out, the two of them went to the public access landing area, and the man had John practice loading and unloading the boat. By the time John got home with the new boat and got it backed up the drive, it was 2. Excited about the boat, he called Debbie and invited her and her family to a day of cruising down the river, fishing and picnicking.

Debbie thought it was a great idea, but only after church. Another problem she thought of was that none of them had a fishing license or the gear for it.

"Okay, no problem," John laughed. "We'll meet for supper tonight at the Asian Buffet next to the sporting goods store and kill two birds with a single stone."

"I don't know if we can afford that, Dad."

"My treat," John insisted.

"Okay," Debbie surrendered. "6 okay?"

"Perfect. See you then." John felt pretty good about himself as he closed his cell phone and walked around the boat. Then he thought about the dishes waiting to be returned. "Well, I'm on a roll, might as well get that out of the way." He told himself.

When Stephanie opened the front door after his second ringing of the doorbell, she was a far cry from the well-dressed woman that had dropped the dishes off. She was dressed in a cotton, button-down blouse, worn blue jeans, and bare-footed. Her hair was pulled back and 90% had been captured with a rubber band, but that remaining 10% was doing its best Einstein impression. She had little or no makeup on, and looked tired and her eyes looked swollen.

John thanked her for the food as he handed the clean dishes back to her.

"Was it okay?" She asked, but didn't seem too interested in his reply.

"It was wonderful," John replied, then paused a moment and looked into her sad eyes. "Are you okay, Stephanie?"

She looked at him for a long moment, then nodded her head. "Yeah, I'm fine."

John didn't move. He held her eyes in his. He could tell that she was saying one thing and meaning another. "Are you sure?"

She started to say yes, but the words stumbled and he could see that she was on the verge of tears.

"Want to talk?"

She hesitated for a moment. "Would you like a cup of coffee?"

"I would enjoy that very much."

She smiled a sad smile and motioned with a nod of her head for him to come in and follow her. It was a modest home, but well appointed, and certainly bigger than a single woman would need. The kitchen was modern, efficient and completely spotless. A commercial type Bunn® coffee maker sat on the counter next to the large double sink. She quickly inserted a filter and four scoops of ground beans, hit the switch and instantly the coffee started brewing.

"Internally plumbed?" John asked, impressed.

Stephanie gave an almost pained laugh. "That was my Bill, always into the latest and greatest. This coffee pot cost more than our first car."

"You miss him terribly," John said more than asked.

Stephanie looked at him a moment without a reply. Then she started to say something and stopped before the utterance of the first word. She seemed to think another second. "It's far more complicated than that."

"Meaning?" John asked, then added. "If you are uncomfortable talking about this to me, I understand."

Stephanie looked into his eyes for a moment, then glanced over at the brewing coffee pot. She didn't reply right off, instead, she pulled two stoneware cups from the cupboard and filled both full of steaming rich, black coffee.

She nodded to the little breakfast nook in the corner of the large kitchen. "Let's have a seat."

Once they had seated themselves across from one another, Stephanie looked at him with her big sad eyes and feigned a slight smile. "You mind starting this conversation by telling me about you and Janice."

"What do you want to know?"

"Were you happy?"

"Of course," John instantly replied, then thought about it a bit deeper. "We really were. We were not always

38

aware of that, nor did we appreciate it as we should have, but we really were. We had the typical struggles all couples have, mostly about money or the kids, which in our case were our two daughters. Jan didn't believe in spanking."

"And you did."

John laughed. "I don't know if it was a belief, but it was how I was raised. If you were bad, or disrespectful, you paid the price. I accepted that there was a price to be paid for bad behavior."

"So who was right?" Stephanie asked. "Your girls are grown now, and they turned out good, right?"

"Yes, and yes, they did." John conceded. "That isn't the case in other families though. I think that is part of the problem with society. We have a whole generation that has grown up not knowing that there is a price for bad behavior."

"That's a topic for another day," Stephanie nodded. "All in all, you two were happy."

"Yes," John answered. "Even more so in the last ten years."

"Why was that?"

John thought a second to arrange his answer to that. "A number of reasons really. The biggest of which, I believe, was that our faith grew stronger, and because of that, our appreciation for what we had, our level of comfort, not in material things, but in ourselves and each other. I think we began to really notice the values in each other. In Jan, I really began to take notice of the many, many talents she had for arts and crafts."

"Not to mention her gardening ability," Stephanie noted with admiration in her voice.

"Absolutely," John smiled. "Which is a source of concern for me right now."

"Why?"

"This is going to sound crazy, but I see those flowers as a living part of her."

"Aww, I think that is beautiful," Stephanie smiled.

"But, what if I can't keep them alive and flourishing as she did?"

"You'll do just fine, I am sure."

"You think?" John frowned. "I watered them the other night. Then I got to wondering, how much water do they need before I am just drowning them? And what about weeding them? I looked them over closely and to be honest, I don't know which are good plants and which are weeds. Not all of them have flowers, you know."

Stephanie laughed, it looked good on her. "You are just going to have to learn something of gardening."

"Oh great," John frowned. "Maybe a night class at the community college on botany."

"Or get help from a friend that can teach you what you need to know," Stephanie replied.

John didn't reply to that, choosing to switch the subject. "What about you and Bill, were you happy?"

Stephanie looked into John's eyes a moment, then got up and brought the coffee pot over to refill their cups.

When she had returned the pot to the coffee maker, she slid back into the nook and sadly looked into her cup. "We were very happy at first," Stephanie started without lifting her eyes from the coffee cup. "We had big plans for a great big, wonderful life. Filled with beautiful things and lots of children. Bill had a good education and a great job making really good money. We could buy anything we wanted, except the ability to have children."

"I am sorry." John had his first glimpse into her heart.

"At first, we just kept trying," Stephanie smiled. "Then we searched for medical answers, I was barren, and Bill didn't want to adopt. So we started going on really nice and expensive vacations. We traveled through Europe and took cruises. Always had nice things, new cars or whatever we wanted. I thought it was his way of dealing with the real issue, but he just said that we didn't have to worry about leaving a big estate."

"Doesn't sound like a bad life," John noted.

"It really wasn't," Stephanie agreed. "But in time, I turned to reading while Bill turned to watching football and other such things on television."

"And gadgets," John tried to inject a little humor.

"Yes, and gadgets. Lots of gadgets. Bill loved his gadgets." Stephanie smiled, then grew silent for a moment. "Do you remember an old country song that raised the question of love being more habit than desire?"

John thought a moment. "I don't recall the song per sè, but I do remember a song with that sentiment."

"Well, that describes our marriage," Stephanie admitted. "We each lived our life in our little world and accepted the other for the benefit they brought to that existence. Bill made good money so I could shop for the things I liked and buy lots of food and drink. He kept me in a life that I was comfortable in. I kept his house clean and food ready for him when he got home from work; did laundry and paid the bills so he didn't have to worry about anything outside of his work. When he was home, he could relax and watch television while I sat in a chair across the room reading my novels. Our life together was a habit formed over the years."

"But you weren't happy?"

"I didn't really think much about it until Bill died," Stephanie replied. "The funny thing was, being alone wasn't that much of a change. That realization really hit me hard. Made me realize that here I am almost 60 years old and that I've gone through life living alone with a man that I met over 40 years before."

John stared into her eyes not knowing what to say to that.

"Oh there were the occasional tender moments," Stephanie was reading his thoughts. "But it was all routine. The same each time. The same day and time, like we were on a schedule or something."

John still didn't know what to say, so he just listened.

"I didn't think about it then, but after he was gone I realized that in the last 20 years of our life together, he never told me that he loved me, or even said that I looked

42

nice. Not once did he reach out and just tenderly touch me, give me a hug, or tell me what I meant to him."

"Wow, I am so sorry," John finally said. "I am sure he felt it, maybe he just couldn't say the words. Some people are that way."

"It's not just the words, but actions as well." Stephanie frowned. "I realize now that I was just one of his gadgets. I actually thought all couples were like that after so many years together."

"What changed your mind about that?"

Stephanie smiled, "Janice did actually."

"She did?"

"Yes. One day I stopped and chatted with her while she was gardening along the fence in front of your house. We had a lovely chat, and I really enjoyed her. So whenever I saw her out and about in the yard, I would come over and we would talk. Sometimes we had coffee or iced tea."

"I had no idea," John didn't mask his surprise. "Funny that in that time I never met you."

"Oh, you did. A couple of times in fact."

"Really?"

"Guess I didn't make much of an impression."

"I'm terribly sorry. Like I told you before, I tend to get lost in my own little world. I suppose in many ways like your Bill did. Maybe, it's a guy thing."

"Maybe it is," Stephanie conceded. "The difference is that you included Janice in that little world of yours. You always told her how beautiful she was, made silly, corny passes at her."

"She told you that?"

"She did. She always said that she never went a day without you touching her, hugging her, and telling her you loved her."

John was nodding and looking into his nearly empty coffee cup. It made him feel good to hear that his signs of affection had meant so much to Jan.

"Bill did none of those things," Stephanie said. "I can't even remember the last time he complimented the way I looked."

"The human race is much like snowflakes," John replied. "None of us are the same. I'm sure he felt for you as I did for Jan. His way was just different than mine. I once heard a story about an old couple where the woman asked the man if he loved her? He said that he had told her years ago that he did. Not happy with that answer, the woman asked why he hadn't told her that in years. His reply was that he had told her once, and he would inform her if there was a change in that area."

"We still need to hear it."

"It would be great if we did tell the people that mean the most to us how we feel, but it doesn't always happen. Do you think he didn't love you?"

44

"Oh, I don't know." She answered. "All I know is that lately I have been feeling alone, depressed and like the world is passing me by."

"Can I make a suggestion?"

"Of course."

"Don't sit here alone in this house, get out and mingle with other people. Find where others our age go. Do something besides sit here alone reading novels." John said, then quickly asked a question, "What kind of novels do you read?"

"Romance novels."

"Well, there's the problem," John teased. "The idiots that write those things have no clue about the real world."

"Oh they do too," Stephanie actually laughed. "They certainly know how the women of the world would like real life to be."

"If the world was like a romance novel, mankind would have died out long ago."

"And why is that?" Stephanie was enjoying this conversation now.

"We would have over-populated, and while we were procreating, who would have been planting crops and supplying food?"

Stephanie laughed out loud at that. "You may have a point."

John looked at his watch, they had been talking for over an hour. "I thank you for the hospitality, and the lasagna was incredible. Thank you."

"It was my pleasure," Stephanie got to her feet and took John's empty cup and placed them both in the sink. "I am glad you stopped by, it brightened my day."

"I enjoyed our little talk as well, and remember you need to spend more time out and about and less time reading those junk novels."

"I'll keep that in mind," Stephanie laughed. "I'll try getting out more, but give up my novels, not a chance!"

John just shook his head.

"One thing I have learned," Stephanie turned serious. "As you cope with living alone, there will be good and bad moments. If you need an ear, just call me."

"You do the same," John gave her a quick hug and took his leave.

7

On his walk home, John's mind was going a hundred miles a minute. He felt like he was being pulled into a situation he wasn't ready for, and not even sure he was up to handling. Stephanie was a wonderful lady, even beautiful, kind, and fun to talk to. He knew in his heart that he had married the love of his life. Jan had been his perfect partner, his lover and best friend. If he ever was ready for another relationship, he knew he would always compare the new woman to his beautiful Jan. If wouldn't be fair, but no woman would ever live up to that standard.

Maybe he was reading too much into this. Maybe Stephanie just needed a friend to talk to. Maybe she would heed his advice and get out with others her age and find that someone. If so, then this situation would take care of itself. If not, he knew he would have to make it clear that he was not ready, and might never be. He didn't want it to get to that point. He knew it would hurt Stephanie, and she had endured enough pain.

All of it was beyond his control at the moment, and he had other things to focus on, like the new boat. He quickly made his way up the driveway so he could unhook the boat from the truck and meet Debbie and her family at the restaurant at 6. Just as he was about to unhook the trailer, he had another thought. "Why unhook the boat when he could just take Jan's car?" He liked that idea, and left the boat and trailer hooked to the truck and went in the house to do a few chores before showering for supper.

The Asian Buffet was only fifteen minutes from his house so when he came out the back door at 5:30, he wasn't in a rush. He climbed behind the wheel of Jan's car and was about to start it when he thought he caught a slight whiff of that perfume Jan loved to wear. He stopped in mid-breath, his heart sinking. He lightly ran his fingers over the leather-wrapped steering wheel. The same wheel Jan had held for over ten years. The car was getting old, but she had always taken such good care of it, that it looked like new. It was an extension of her. No matter how old it got, it always looked its best. Just as Jan always had. He got back out of the car and locked it before going back into the house and getting his pickup keys.

He had to hurry to the restaurant. Not unhooking the boat earlier in the day had cost him time when he could ill afford it. Sure enough, when he pulled into the restaurant's parking lot, Debbie and her family were all there standing next to their car waiting for his arrival.

"Was beginning to worry about you," Debbie said as he got out. "Being late isn't something I've ever seen from you."

"Long story, best saved for another time," John said as he hugged her tightly.

As was always the case, Asian Buffet was a gluttonous feast. Little J.J. discovered that he loved shrimp. John watched in total fascination as the little guy put them away. Grant ate quietly, only giving short one or two-word answers to anything John asked him, but when J.J. had finished the shrimp on his plate, Grant was on his feet getting more for him.

They left the cars in the restaurant's parking lot and walked over to the sporting goods store. Everyone but J.J. would need a license and, at least two poles. Then there was tackle, nets, pole holders, life vests and bait to buy. The salesperson was very helpful, especially when it came to buying anchors for the boat. John wanted to be able to anchor off in the middle of the river. He ended up with four anchors of the fluted design that were strong and yet light enough that Debbie could handle them if need be.

The following morning Debbie called at 11:45 to say that they were ready to go and that she had lunch. They met at the local park that offered a place to launch boats into the river. It was a beautiful day and, surprisingly, there were very few people about. Jason and Grant helped get the boat into the water without incident. While John went to park the truck and trailer, the supplies were loaded onto the boat. Everything went well until J.J. was lifted up on deck. Instantly, he went running across the deck with a gleeful shriek and in seconds found a way to swing open one of the rail gates and fall into the water. Before anyone could react, Grant was in the water pulling a choking J.J. out and handing him up to his terrified mother.

The day almost ended right there. Debbie had second thoughts about this whole idea. Grant argued that all they had to do was secure the gates so J.J. couldn't open them.

"And just how are you going to do that?" His mother wanted to know.

"Simple," Grant replied while grabbing one of the four anchors. "We are not going to need four anchors, not today anyway. We just take this anchor line and cut it into four lengths and tie the four gates shut so he can't open them."

Debbie just looked at Grant, and then her husband, and finally her father. John just nodded in Grant's direction signaling that he agreed with that solution. "What about your wet clothes? J.J. is soaked."

"We'll dry, and he doesn't seem to mind," Grant answered, pointing to a once again happy J.J. running around the deck checking everything out.

The river was so peaceful and beautiful. Any misgivings Debbie harbored about this little family outing were soon lost to the splendor of the scenery. After motoring upstream for half an hour, John decided that it was time to try the fishing. Grant handled the bow anchors while Jason handled the lone stern anchor. As soon as the boat came to rest against her anchors, John decided to raise the canopy to shelter two-thirds of the boat's deck from the sun.

Grant was amazing with little J.J. He taught him the basics of casting, and J.J. seemed to love doing that, although his casts were a danger to himself and everyone aboard. J.J. hated the worms, but cried when he reeled his line in and the worm had gotten off. He cried again when a fish took his bait and the line suddenly jerked. The jerk scared J.J. so he dropped the pole and before Grant could grab it, the fish yanked it into the water and it was gone. John listened proudly as Grant explained to J.J. that he had to hold on to the pole. That poor fish was probably doomed with that pole attached to it. Luckily, they had gotten two poles for J.J. and he was back to fishing in no time.

When Grant got a bite, he quickly set the hook, then had J.J. help him reel the fish in. Little J.J. wasn't sure what to make of what was happening. His wide eyes and facial expressions had his parents and grandfather in stitches. When they did manage to land the fish, J.J. was in total amazement. As the fish laid on the deck of the boat, J.J.

went close to it, and with his hands on his knees, bent down close to get a really good look at the slimy creature they had just pulled from the river. When the fish suddenly flipped over, little J.J. ran behind his brother's legs, cautiously peering out between Grant's legs at the flopping demon of the deep.

He was also amazed when Grant picked the fish up with a finger through the gills and deftly removed the embedded hook. Debbie wanted a picture of the boys with their catch, but J.J. wouldn't come out from between Grant's legs. He felt that he was close enough to that thing. As soon as Debbie got the best picture she could, Grant released the fish and J.J. stood there waving bye-bye to it.

While Jason and the boys were enjoying their fishing, Debbie sat close to her father and they talked. John told her about his visit with Stephanie and his concerns about that. Debbie agreed that he had reason to be concerned, but he was smart enough to not get reeled into a situation he was uncomfortable with.

I don't blame her for trying," Debbie laughed.

"Why do you say that?"

"You'd be quite a catch Dad," Debbie answered. "Mom wasn't the easiest person to live with and yet you seemed to manage."

"Your mother wasn't so tough to live with," John argued.

"Because you learned how to handle her ways." Debbie pointed. "Just as she learned to handle you. Mom was passive-aggressive. She seemed easy-going on the outside, but she wasn't going to do anything she didn't want to."

"We're all like that."

"Maybe, but Mom had her ways. Wendy will agree with me on that. Sometimes we wondered how you coped with her moods."

"The only thing I worried about where your mother was concerned was when someone interrupted her routine."

"Oh she was a creature of habit." Debbie laughed.

The entire day was a wonderful family time. Neither John nor Debbie ever got a hook wet, choosing instead to talk and laugh together. For their picnic time, John pulled the boat under a large tree growing on the edge of the water and Grant and Jason secured the anchors. Little J.J. kept them all laughing as he rambled on in gibberish about all he had seen and done. And he didn't stop talking until they had the boat loaded and the little guy strapped into his car seat, and he suddenly just fell asleep.

8

The following morning John was up before the sun. He made his way into the kitchen and hit the button to start the coffee brewing. Then he grabbed his notebook and a good ink pen and sat down to start his to-do list. About five minutes later he got up, went to the cupboard, pulled out a cup, turned toward the coffee maker and realized that nothing had happened since he hadn't set it up the night before. He looked up to the ceiling, "oh quit laughing Jan, coffee pot prep was your job."

He made the coffee and got back to his list. He felt like he had two top priorities that day. The first was to clean the boat up from the day before. The second, call the local community college and see if he could hire a botany teacher or student to advise him on the flower gardens. He somehow felt that the gardens were a living legacy of the woman he loved more than life. He had to keep them as she left them. Not only alive but thriving. As he sat there thinking about that, he suddenly had another thought. Jan spent a great deal of her free time tending to her flowers. He suddenly wondered if the task actually required that much effort, or was she just idling her time away where she felt so at peace?

The coffee was finally ready. He filled his cup, and not feeling like eating yet, slipped on a light jacket and went outside to inspect the boat. He started the truck and pulled the boat far enough down the drive so that the water from washing it would run down the drive to the street and into the storm drain. After five minutes of spraying the deck with the hose, he realized that the boat was far dirtier than plain water would clean. He shut the hose off and went back inside to retrieve a bucket and some soap.

He had just stepped into the house when his cell phone rang. He pulled it out of his pocket and noticed it was Debbie's work number. The phone was an old style flip-phone, so he flipped it open and greeted his daughter.

"Good morning darling."

"Well, it was," Debbie didn't sound happy.

"Oh-oh, what's wrong?"

"I just got a call from Grant's school. They want me to come right down and pick my son up."

"Oh, and why is that?" John felt irritation rising in his heart. Grant just couldn't seem to fit in and go along with what society expected of him.

"He is being expelled for two weeks." Debbie's voice betrayed that she was on the verge of tears.

"How can I help?" John realized that his little girl needed him right now, and that was more important than anything else.

"Would you mind going and getting him?" Debbie asked. "I just got here, and can't possibly ask them to let me go. This type of thing has happened way too much with Grant. I need to keep my job."

"I'll go get him," John assured her. "Why is he being expelled? He just got back from being expelled last week."

"I know Dad," Debbie's voice was starting to break. The strain of Grant's behavior was taking its toll on her. "All they would tell me on the phone is that it is for fighting. I'm sorry Dad, I just can't deal with it right now."

"Don't worry about it, I'll go get him," John said. "You want him dropped off at home?"

"No! Can you keep him with you? I'll pick him up after work. Maybe I'll be able to handle it then."

"Okay, he can help me clean the boat."

"That would be fine, but don't take him fishing. No rewards for his behavior."

"I understand. Don't worry." John soothed her.

"I'll let the school know that you'll be there to get him soon."

"Okay great. Don't worry about anything and we'll see you tonight." John flipped the phone closed and rubbed the back of his neck. He would give anything to understand that boy. He refilled his coffee cup and then returned to the boat. There was nothing to be done about it. He backed the boat and trailer up the drive to its parking space in front of the garage and unhooked it.

On the drive to the school, he kept running ideas through his mind on how he might reach out to Grant. The fact was, he felt like grabbing the boy by the shoulders and shaking him to wake him up to what he was doing to himself and those around him that loved him. When he arrived at the school, Grant was sitting in the outer office by himself. Grant looked up and said "Hi Papa," when John stepped into the office. The school secretary asked John to sign Grant out, which he did, but before leaving, John asked to speak with the Principal. He was ushered into the inner office and introduced to a young man in his mid-thirties, dressed in a cheap navy blue suit, white shirt, and red tie.

55

The Principal went into why Grant was being expelled. The three boys he had beaten up were the same three he had threatened and had received a three day expulsion for, just last week. The Principal cited that as proof that Grant had learned nothing from last week's expulsion and had come to school that morning with every intention of carrying out his threat from last week.

John's point of view was that in his time, kids were allowed to settle their differences amongst themselves. It was important because it taught them how to get along once out of school. In the real world, there would not be anyone to step in.

"That is what the police do." The Principal pointed out. "Besides, the school has a no tolerance rule, and Grant had broken that rule twice in as many weeks. If, when his two-week suspension was over, he returned and found himself in trouble again, he would be expelled for the balance of the school year. Then he would have to go before the school board to be allowed back in the next year."

"Where are the other boys that were involved in the fight?" John wanted to know.

"In class."

"Why are they not being punished?"

The Principal looked like he was getting tired of this discussion. "They weren't involved in the fight other than to be Grant's victims. None of them even threw a punch."

John could see that talking with this guy was pointless, so he just nodded and walked out of the inner

56

office and collected Grant. He waited until they were in his truck and pulling out of the school parking lot before asking Grant what had happened. Grant's reply was simple and straight forward. He had decked a couple of punks.

"Who threw the first punch?" John asked.

"I threw the only punches," Grant replied. "Three of them, and the fight was over. Wasn't really a fight, more of a lesson."

"They didn't even throw a punch?"

"No," Grant replied. "They didn't have a chance to, and why would I let them?"

"You can't just beat people up," John scolded him. "Not in school or out here in the real world."

"You have to stand up for yourself," Grant responded. "It's the only way punks learn."

"So they started it by verbally assaulting you?"

"Sort of."

"Sort of? What kind of answer is that?" John asked. "They either did or they didn't."

"They're just always talking crap, and I got tired of it and told them to shut up." Grant replied. "When they asked who was going to make them, I told them I would. That was what a teacher heard last week. Today they started their trash talking again, so I just shut them up."

"Oh, my God," John sighed.

"Just let it go Papa," Grant said. "It's over."

"It's not over," John argued. "The school is going to be watching you very closely when you go back. If you step over the line for any reason, you'll be out for the rest of the year."

From there the conversation went downhill fast, so much so that by the time they got to John's house the two of them were barely talking. Despite that, they went to work on washing the boat. Over the course of the next hour, things seemed to work themselves out. By the time they were drying the boat off, the two of them were chatting and laughing about silly things. Just as they were pulling the heavy cloth cover over the boat, Stephanie walked up the driveway.

"Nice boat." She smiled.

"Thanks," John replied while motioning toward Grant. "This is my grandson, Grant. Grant, this is my neighbor Stephanie."

"Pleased to meet you," Grant nodded toward her.

"Nice to meet such a polite and handsome young man," Stephanie smiled. "You look just like your grandfather."

John and Grant exchanged a quick glance.

"I found this book in my collection," Stephanie said as she pulled a hard-bound book from her purse. "It's all about flowers and taking care of flower gardens. Just thought you might like to have it." She stepped closer to John and offered the book to him.

"Oh, wow!" John said as he accepted the book and quickly flipped through the pages of photographs. "I might be able to save her gardens with this."

"Wouldn't hurt to talk with a botanist anyway, but I thought it would make a great reference tool," Stephanie smiled. "Well, I won't keep you boys from your work. Enjoy your day."

"Thank you," John didn't really know what else to say. "This is very kind of you. Thank you."

"Oh, it's nothing, have fun reading." Stephanie turned and slowly walked back down the drive and turned toward her home.

The two watched her go. Then after she had stepped out of sight, Grant looked at his grandfather. "She likes you." John just looked at him without comment. "Did you hear her call me handsome?" Grant continued. "Then say just like you. She didn't call you handsome directly, but she said it."

John just frowned and then held the book up. "Let's get this job finished and then go see if we can identify some flowers."

They had identified a dozen or so different flowers in Jan's gardens by the time Debbie pulled into the drive. She was clearly angry with Grant and just asked him to get into the car. When Grant closed the car door, Debbie turned to her father and asked how things went with her errant son.

"May I ask you a favor?" John asked instead of answering her question.

"Sure, what?"

"Let me work on Grant for the next two weeks. See if I can get inside his head. If you two get into a fight over this, nothing will be accomplished. So leave it be. Let me see what I can do with the boy."

Debbie stood silent for a moment before nodding her acceptance. "I'm not really up to a fight right now anyway. You have a deal." She hugged her father and got into the car and backed down the drive.

9

John was on his second pot of coffee by the time Debbie pulled into the drive and escorted Grant into the house.

"What are you two going to do today?" She asked with suspicion.

"We've got the boat all cleaned up." Grant suggested.

"No fishing," Debbie answered firmly.

"Guess we leave the poles behind," John replied.

"No fishing and no boating." Debbie remained firm. "This is not a time of reward."

"What did I do?" John teased.

Debbie looked at him a long moment, trying to read his thoughts. "I'll get back to you on that."

"All right," John conceded. "The boat remains parked. We'll just have to spend the day figuring out what flowers your mother planted and how to care for them."

"Sounds like a good plan, that'll keep the two of you busy." Debbie gave her dad a light kiss on the cheek and then gave Grant one as well. "I expect you both to stay out of trouble. And Grant…"

"Yes?"

"Listen to your grandfather."

"Yes, ma'am."

Once Debbie had left, John offered Grant some coffee, which he readily accepted saying that his mother doesn't let him have it. "She thinks I am too young for it."

"Really?"

"Yes, really."

John shrugged. "I was drinking coffee with my grandfather at age six or seven. Liked a lot of cream and sugar in it then, black now. How do you like yours?"

Grant smiled sheepishly. "With lots of cream and sugar, just like Grandma used to make it for me."

John paused a sad nostalgic moment, then nodded. "I'll let you fix it then. I never made it to suit her." John got a second cup out of the cupboard and then filled it with hot coffee. He slid the sugar bowl over to it, and then reached into the refrigerator and grabbed the carton of cream. "Want a bagel?"

"No, I'm good." Grant replied as he dumped four teaspoons of sugar and all the cream the cup would hold into the coffee. John had already returned to the table and was thumbing through the gardening book looking at all the different kinds of flowers. "There is something we could do today besides work on the gardens." Grant offered.

"Oh, and what is that?"

"The tractor." Grant replied.

"What about the tractor?"

"Restore it." Grant answered. "You said that you always wanted to restore it." He let that sink in before continuing. "We've got two weeks, and it would be something that should take about that long. And it would be a cool guy thing to do."

John only had to think about it for a second. He had been wondering what they were going to do to fill their time, especially since Debbie had taken the boat out of the picture. "Okay, the tractor it is."

"Cool." Grant smiled as he took a seat at the table next to his grandfather.

John took up his notebook and flipped the started to-do list to a fresh page.

"What is that for?" Grant asked.

"The 5 p's," John replied, which left Grant without a clue to his meaning. "The 5 p's are this: Prior Planning Prevents Poor Performance."

"That's cool, I like that."

"First things first," John said, and he started the list. "We have to make room for the project in the middle of the garage. That means getting the truck and car out of there. To accomplish this, the boat will have to be moved."

Grant nodded his agreement. "Also," John continued. "I suspect that we'll create a lot of dust, so I want to be sure we move the boat and your grandmother's car far enough away to keep them from catching all that dust."

They carefully laid out a detailed 34 item to-do list for that day. It took over an hour to get the vehicles and boat moved out of the way and the dead tractor with three flat tires to the middle of the garage. Two of the tires inflated just fine, but the third was losing air almost as fast as they could put it in, and John had a pretty good air

63

compressor. They would fill the tire and move the tractor about a foot before needing to re-inflate the tire.

The first thing they needed to accomplish was to remove the sheet metal, meaning the hood, fenders, grille, and such from the tractor. Not an easy task with the tools they had. John had plenty of tools, just not many big enough to be working on a tractor. He realized early on that to do the job right, they would have to make a list of what tools they would need and then make a tool run. They would need a heavy jack, 4 strong jack stands, and angle grinders with both grinding and wire wheels. He had a lot of 3/8" drive tools, but he needed heavier ½" drive sockets and air wrenches. They made their list and jumped into the truck.

Two hours later, they were back and unloading the truck. John had spent more than he would have liked, but had truly enjoyed shopping for tools with Grant. They got the tractor up on four jack stands and removed the tires and wheels and then separated the rear hubs from the rims. Then all the sheet metal, the rims and hubs and front wheels were loaded into the truck. They first went to the tire dealer and had the old tires removed from the rims, and then went to a commercial sand blaster and dropped everything off.

When they got back to the garage, they pulled out a couple of lawn chairs, and a couple of sodas from the old refrigerator John kept in the garage. They sat down and looked at the stripped carcass of the old tractor.

"So what's next?" Grant asked.

John thought a moment, "We'll need to drain all the fluids out of her, and then we need to remove the wiring, oil lines, throttle linkage, belts, radiator and that kind of thing before we pull the engine."

"How do you know how to do all of this?" Grant asked.

"I'm a genius, didn't your mother tell you?"

"No, seriously." Grant laughed.

"I'm serious. If you don't believe it, just ask me."

"Papa, that doesn't make any sense." Grant was shaking his head.

"Well, I grew up on a farm. There was always something in need of fixing. I guess I was blessed with an ability to look something over and figure out how it works. Kind of the same way your grandmother could look at a plant and know what it needed to flourish." John answered.

"How did you two meet?" Grant asked.

"We went to school together but didn't really know each other. " John suddenly had a far-away look in his eyes as he remembered their first true meeting. "It was the last school dance of our senior year. She had come with a guy she had been dating. I had gone alone, hoping to find a girl."

"I can understand that." Grant laughed

"Anyway, unknown to your grandmother, her boyfriend had his eyes on another, and this other girl decided that she wanted your grandmother's date. He had gotten up from their table to get some punch. That other girl approached him at the refreshment counter. Your grandmother saw it happening, yet remained at their table.

Then the crowd of kids on the dance floor blocked her view, and when the line-of-sight cleared, both her date and the girl were gone. She gave it a few minutes and when he didn't come back, she went looking for him."

"Did she find him?"

"Oh yeah, in that other girl's embrace." John nodded. "She let them have it, verbally. When she came back into the gym I noticed she was upset and on the verge of tears. I instantly went over to her and asked if I could help. She told me no at first. I asked her if she was sure. I think I said something like; 'I'm a pretty good listener.' Just as she was about to tell me to get lost, the DJ put a slow, romantic song on. I never could fast dance, and at the time it seemed like God was working in His good old mysterious ways, so I asked her to dance."

"And she said yes." Grant was into the story, although John was sure he had heard it all before.

"She wasn't going to, in fact, years later she told me that she meant to say no, it just didn't come out that way."

"Really?"

"That's what she told me," John assured. "As we were holding each other close and slowly swaying to the soft music, emotion overtook her and she began to cry. I gently put one hand on the back of her head and laid it on my shoulder while rubbing her back tenderly while we danced. As fate would have it, that was the last dance of the night, and as soon as the strains of music began to fade away, the overhead lights began to snap on. She didn't want anyone to see her streaked make-up, so she took my hand and quickly lead me out of the gym. While we were exiting the school, she asked me if I could give her a ride

66

home. She said that she seemed to have lost the ride she came with."

"Boy, she bounced back quickly." Grant noted.

"Oh, she was still plenty upset. In fact, she would have just walked home, but it was over two miles, and she was in heels."

"Grams in heels?" Grant was surprised.

"Oh yeah, she wore those silly feet deformers back then. All the girls did. I agreed to take her home, then remembered that I had driven my dad's farm truck to the dance. I kept apologizing all the way to the truck. When we got to it, I had to half lift her up so she could get into it, and boy did she look and feel heavenly in that satin green dress. The moonlight reflected off her curly red hair, and I was trying so hard not to touch her in any inappropriate places and still get her lifted into the cab of the truck, which wasn't easy."

"How big was the truck?" Grant wanted to know.

"Not really that big, just a ton job with a flat-bed and wooden stake sides. It was just taller than she could manage in that full-length gown. Then once I got her into the cab, she had to get her legs past the floor shift. I kept apologizing for the truck until she said to stop. She noted that it ran and was clean, which it was, and that was all that mattered to her."

"Grams never was into hot cars, was she?"

"She never was," John smiled. "She always seemed grateful for what she had, and never envious of what others had. I never heard her say that she wanted something. The closest she ever got to that was saying <u>something was nice,</u> or that <u>is a pretty car.</u> Never saying that she wanted one of those, whatever it was. She was truly an amazing woman."

"Yes, she was," Grant agreed. "So continue the story, I want to hear how you got your first date."

"I'm sure your mother has told you this story before." John countered.

"She has, but I want to hear it from you."

John <u>looked at him a moment,</u> and then smiled and continued. "So there we were riding towards her home in silence. She didn't feel like talking, and I couldn't figure out what to say. The only time she said anything was to tell me where to turn. The closer we got to her house, the more pressure I felt to say something. Then just as we pulled up to the curb in front of her house and she thanked me for the dance and the ride home, I quickly asked her if she would like to go out to dinner and see a movie Saturday night. She <u>looked at me a moment,</u> then asked if I meant the next night? She didn't say 'it being Friday, and all'. I said yes, she told me later that she could see how nervous I was, and that concerned her a little."

"Women like confident men." Grant acknowledged.

"Yes, yes they do." John agreed. "She thanked me for asking but said that she had had enough of dating for the time being. Before I could say anything else, she opened the passenger door and slid off the seat and right out the door. Before slamming the door shut, she stuck her head back in the cab and thanked me again for the dance, and the ride home."

"Is that when the roses started, that same night?"

68

"Yes indeed. My mother had several large rose bushes that always flourished around the house yard, and that year they were overly abundant. I knew deep in my heart that I had already fallen for your grandmother and started thinking of ways to draw her attention to me. For some reason, I felt sure that if I could get her to give me a chance, I would make her happy. So as I drove out to the farm that night, I kept thinking of different angles to get to her heart. It wasn't until I was pulling into the farm that I noticed the roses. I stopped the truck and quickly searched the glovebox for something I could cut with. My dad always had basic tools in his vehicles. Sure enough, I pulled a pair of diagonal wire cutters out and quickly set about gathering a dozen of the best-looking roses for her."

"Don't roses close up at night or something?" Grant asked.

"Yes, they do, but you can see from the bud which ones are the most beautiful, and I picked only the best. As soon as I had them, I went into the barn and carefully tied some twine around them. We raised purebred hogs then, and Dad always had business cards in the truck. So I took one of the cards and wrote on the back of it, thanks for the best dance of my life, John."

"Mom says that you snuck into town that night and parked a block away and secretly left the flowers on her back door." Grant said.

"Your mother is right about that," John smiled. "Except it was the side door. The one I watched her go through when I had dropped her off, so I knew it was the door the family used regularly."

"So she had a business card," Grant was putting an idea together in his mind. "That means she had your phone number and a way of thanking you for the flowers, but she didn't."

"No she didn't, and yes she could have." John agreed.

"So you did it again the next night."

"And every night thereafter for two straight weeks."

"Wow! You were in love." Grant laughed.

"I thought so too," John laughed. "And my mother thought so too. That's why she let me raid her precious rose bushes every night without saying anything, at least until the last night."

"What did Great-Grandma say?" Grant was curious, he couldn't remember the woman.

"When I got home from the last flower run, I had already decided that she was intentionally ignoring me, and to continue was doing nothing more than making a fool of myself."

"Did that make you sad?"

John looked Grant in the eyes and nodded. "It really did, I was so smitten with your grandmother that I could think of nothing else. The picture of her in my arms drove me on when common sense should have pulled me back. Every morning when I went out to do chores I would look at the rose bushes and see the carnage I was inflicting."

"Wow!"

70

"On the way home that last night of delivering the flowers, I decided that was it. I had given it all I could, and I was still not the one she wanted. I couldn't change that, and by that time, there weren't many roses left anyway. As I came into the house, my mother was waiting for me. Somehow she seemed to know the whole story, not who the girl was, but that I was trying to win some girl's heart. She also knew it wasn't working."

"How did she know that?"

"I was never gone long enough." John laughed. "I was gone only long enough to drive into town and right back, so she knew I was just leaving them on the doorstep. And one day, while I was out in the field, she went through the truck and found the business cards, the twine, and the ink pen I used to sign them with. She checked the truck several times after that and counted the cards and put two and two together."

"Great-Grandma was a smart lady." Grant noted.

"Indeed, she was," John smiled at the thought of his mother's face. "More importantly, she was a gentle, loving woman. She realized that her son was in love alone, and felt his pain so deeply that she allowed him to ravage her beautiful rose bushes."

"In love alone?"

"Yes, it is an old term for when you are in love with someone, but they don't love you back. Hence, in love alone." John explained.

"Ah." Grant nodded his understanding. "So your mother was waiting for you."

"She was indeed. At first, I was surprised. My folks always went to bed early, there were chores to be done at the crack of dawn. When I walked in, she looked at me with a very understanding smile and held her arms out to me. She hadn't hugged me that way in years, and as she held me in her arms she asked, 'The flowers are not working are they?' I just shook my head no. When we stepped back from one another, she looked me in the eyes, 'I am truly sorry honey,' she said. 'Maybe it is time to move on, obviously this isn't the girl God has in mind for you." I simply nodded and apologized for ruining her rose bushes on the failed attempt. I can still see her smile when she said not to worry, they would grow back. And just as I was turning to go up to my bedroom, she added a very funny comment to it. 'If you're lucky, they will have grown back before you find another girl you like.'

That made Grant laugh. "I wish I could have gotten to know Great-Grandma.

"I wish that as well, she dearly loved you. She was there to hold you when you were first born."

"She was?"

"Indeed, and I don't think I ever saw her so proud and happy."

Grant smiled and thought about that. "I wish I could remember it, but what was I when she died, 3?"

"Something like that," John replied, lost in the memories of his mother.

"Okay. Back to our story." Grant urged.

"Well," John thought back through the years to the very next day, after his mother had suggested that he move on. "We were up before the crack of dawn and got the chores done. Then Mom made pancakes and eggs for breakfast. Right after breakfast, my dad and I headed out to the field. He was plowing and I was pulling the disc. I remember the day as being unseasonably warm. I had taken my shirt off, my hair was messed up by the wind, and I was covered in a fine dust. About noon, I spotted a Chevy stationwagon coming down the lane and parking just inside the gate to the field we were working. My dad had finished plowing that field and had just pulled out of the gate when the stationwagon pulled in. I saw him get off his tractor, an Allis Chalmers D17, and go over to the car and talk with the people inside. Then, amazingly, I spotted him waving for me to come over. When I got near the car, my dad met me and told me not to waste too much time. He wanted me to finish this field and then meet him in the ten acres across the creek. I asked him who it was, as I still couldn't see who was in the car. He said some girl wanted to talk to me. I remember he said that with a shrug, but I noticed it in his eyes."

"Noticed what?" Grant was really into the story.

"Pride, I think." John laughed. "I remember thinking at the time that the girl must really be cute for my dad to act like he did."

"And she was." Grant smiled.

"Yes, yes she was. She didn't get out of the car until my dad was almost back to his tractor."

"Were you driving this tractor?" Grant pointed at the stripped skeleton sitting before them.

73

"Do you want to hear this story or not?" John teasingly scolded.

"Last interruption, I promise." Grant quickly replied, and then added. "It was this tractor wasn't it?"

"Yes," John nodded toward the stripped old Ford Jubilee. "It was this tractor. I had just turned the ignition off when the girl got out of the car. She kind of looked nervous."

"Grandma? Nervous?"

John just pointed his finger at Grant to make him remember the promise not to interrupt. "Yes, it was your grandma, and coming out that day to thank me for the flowers was her mother's idea. That was the other person in the car. Of course, I didn't personally meet her that day, other than a mutual wave. She stayed in the car and just watched us."

"I remember feeling so out of place with no shirt on and so dirty. But your grandma didn't seem to mind. In fact, years later she told me that that was what sold her on me. My muscular build and my six-pack."

"Yeah, right."

"Hey, I was in pretty good shape then." John protested.

"If you say so Papa." Grant laughed.

"Anyway, she slowly made her way over to the tractor as I got down and as she neared where I stood, I remember asking her if everything was okay. She smiled and nodded, and finally said that everything was more than okay. She thanked me for the lovely flowers, noting that I must be in trouble with my own mother over that generosity. She and her mother had noticed the stripped rose bushes when they pulled in."

"What did you say to that?"

"I don't know what came over me, I was always so shy around pretty girls, but suddenly I had confidence, or, at least, acted like I did. I told her that Mom had forgiven me when I told her how beautiful I thought she, your grandmother, was. You know, it was funny, but your grandmother suddenly lit up. She started laughing and joking. She scolded me for lying to my own mother. I assured her that I didn't lie, and I thought she was the prettiest girl I had ever seen. I told her that I loved everything about her, the way she tilted her head, and I also pointed it out that she was doing it right then, which made her laugh."

"Did you really mean it, or were you just piling it on?"

"I meant it of course!" John tried to sound offended but failed. "I truly meant that all the days of our lives together. Then she, your grandma, thanked me again. She also noted that the reign of flowers was probably over since it looked like I had stolen all my mother had grown. I admitted that it was. I remember telling her: "We're all out of flowers, but manure I have lots of, I could leave a bucket of that every night if it pleased her."

"What did Grandma do?"

"She laughed hysterically," John replied with a big smile, remembering the moment. "It must have struck her funny bone. It also helped her make a decision, or change her mind entirely."

"What do you mean?" Grant wanted to know.

"When her mother had brought her out to the farm, saying it was the least she could do, your grandmother had intended to do just that, thank me for the flowers and leave it at that. When she got control of herself again from laughing, she looked me in the eyes and asked me if the offer for dinner and a movie was still on?"

"And you said yes."

"Well, not right away," John corrected him.

"Say what?!" Grant couldn't believe it.

"My response went something like this. "I don't know if that movie is still playing there anymore, they only keep the same movie showing for so long, then in comes another. But, I suppose it wouldn't hurt to have dinner and see what was playing, say about 7?" Her face lit up, and she ran over to me and gave me a big hug, and whispered in my ear, 'Saturday at 7 it is.'

"Where did you get such confidence, if you were normally shy around girls?" Grant thought he might have found a flaw in his grandfather's story.

"From your grandmother, Son. That girl always made me feel like more than I was, and she continued to do so the rest of her life."

"And like they say on television, the rest is history." Grant smiled. "I heard you two hit it off right away."

"We did," John remembered. "On that first date, my mother insisted that I take their car instead of that old truck. My father thought I should stick with the truck, it had gotten me that far."

76

Grant laughed at that. "Sounds like something you would say."

"Now you know where that all comes from," John replied.

"Did you take the car?"

"I did, it was a Chevy Nova," John smiled. "When I went to pick her up, I parked at the curb and walked up to the side door and knocked. That is when I met your great-grandmother. I guess she had fallen for me long before her daughter did. She told me that they didn't expect me at the back door, which was for family. Guests used the front door. About a month after we started dating, I was using the back door regularly. It was then I realized that I better propose to that girl before she or her family changed their minds."

"Wow! You got engaged that soon?"

"They became engaged within six weeks of dating," Debbie answered for her father as she came through the side door of the garage. "And were married just five months after the first date."

"Wow! That is amazing. You two got married so quickly and it lasted so long."

"That's because they were the ones God Himself had hand-picked for each other." Debbie answered for her father."

John looked at her with an amused smiled.

"It is what both you and Mom always attributed it to," Debbie replied before he even commented. "You two have been busy. Going to restore Grandpa's old tractor?"

"We sure are," Grant answered proudly. "Did you know Papa was driving this very tractor when he got his first date with Grandma?"

Debbie turned to her father. "Really? I didn't know that part of the story."

"It's true," John replied.

"Well, that's cool." Debbie then turned to Grant. "We better get moving, because I have to get supper going."

"Okay." Grant said getting to his feet, stepping over to John and giving him a hug. "See you in the morning, Papa."

John patted Grant on the back. "Sounds like a plan, thanks again Son, we made good progress today."

"We'll do even better tomorrow," Grant said as he stepped through the side door and out of the garage.

Debbie turned to her father just before she stepped out. "Well?"

John simply gave her the thumbs up sign.

10

John was sitting at the table drinking coffee and filling out the to-do list when Debbie and Grant came through the door. John offered her some coffee, which she turned down. She kissed her father's cheek first and then her son's, and as she went out the door, she reminded them to be good.

"Why does she think I could get into trouble with you?" Grant asked jokingly.

"I don't know," John replied. "Maybe she knows something we don't."

"Or maybe just thinks she knows." Grant corrected.

"Well, she is a woman," John smiled. "If you want coffee, you know where it is, help yourself."

Grant went to the cupboard and pulled out a cup, filled it and added the ton of sugar and cream just like his grandmother used to do. It wasn't until he sat down next to him that John noticed which cup he had taken. "That was your grandmother's favorite cup. Don't believe anyone but she has ever drunk from it."

"Oh, I'm sorry. I'll get another." Grant started to get up before John stopped him.

"No, please. Use the cup. I like the idea of you using it, and I think she would too."

"Okay, thanks." Grant said as he settled back into his chair. "What's it like now for you here?"

"What do you mean?"

"Well," Grant paused to arrange his question in his own mind. "You and Grandma lived here together for many years, right?"

"Almost forty years, yes."

"And now you are here alone. The same walls, the same bed, the same everything. The pictures on the walls are hung where she put them. Grandma was so good at decorating and being crafty. I see her in everything I see in here. Just seeing things the way she made them or arranged them makes me miss her. I can't imagine how it all makes you feel."

John looked at his grandson for a long moment and then glanced around the kitchen. Grant was right, nothing had been changed or moved from where Jan had placed it. "You know, for a kid, you are pretty insightful."

"Thank you."

"And to tell the truth," John let those words linger as he thought a moment and took a deep breath. "I suppose how I feel changes from minute to minute. You are also right in that she had a gift for decorating. She took a simple structure and turned it into an inviting, comfortable place to live. A lot of that was accomplished by her just being in it. Now with her gone, I look around and see and feel her spirit. Her eye for detail continues to be pleasing. Something I have always admired about her gift was that no matter where you looked in here, there was much to see. Little details that were never apparent at first. Every nook and cranny offers something pleasing to the eye."

"I never understood how she could do it like she did." Grant agreed.

"Now, as I walk through the empty house, and look upon her things, I still feel her presence. It's like her spirit is walking with me. I even talk to her sometimes. Crazy isn't it?"

"No, I don't think so at all." Grant replied. "In fact, I had a dream about her last night."

"Really? What was it about?"

"I was in the garage working on the tractor and she came through the door. I knew she was dead, but it seemed so natural, I didn't give it a second thought. She scolded me for ruining my clothes, and then she was gone."

John nearly spit out his mouth full of coffee. "Now that was your grandmother!" he laughed.

As soon as the to-do list was complete, they made their way out to the garage. First, on the list was to carefully look the chassis over for evidence of previous leaks. Not really worrying about the engine, since that was going to be totally rebuilt and would have all new gaskets anyway. The areas they focused on were the hydraulic system and the power-takeoff, and both showed signs of past leakage. John handed the digital camera to Grant and told him to make a clear and complete photographic record of the tractor in her present state. He told him to be sure to get clear pictures of the wiring. While Grant was busy with that, John found a five-gallon bucket and a length of hose to siphon the old gas out of her. Getting the siphon going meant that he would have to create a vacuum by sucking on one end of the hose while the other end was in the fuel tank. He knew what would happen, and it did. He got a mouthful of the old gas that smelled and tasted horrible, almost like turpentine. He spit it out, then coughed and spit some more.

"You okay?" Grant asked worried.

"Just dandy." John coughed out, then spit again into the bucket slowly filling with the nasty old gas.

"Didn't you know that was going to happen?" Grant asked.

"Oh yeah, knew it, and did it anyway." John spit out. "Got to get that nasty stuff out of there, and by the smell and looks of it, we better have the tank boiled out when we get it off of here."

"How's it taste?" Grant asked with a smirk.

"Like aged whiskey gone horribly wrong." John looked at Grant. "Next time you can do the honors."

"I'll find another way, thank you."

While the gas siphoned out of the tank and into the bucket, John busied himself with marking all electrical wires. When Grant finished taking the pictures, John had him start removing the wiring harness. By noon they had removed the fuel tank, all of the engine's externals; like starter, carburetor, manifold, generator and so on. The engine, transmission, and rear end had been drained of fluids and the coolant and radiator removed. Finally, they were able to remove the front axle, radius arms, and tie-rods, and separate the engine from the transmission. At first, the engine was set down on blocks on the garage floor. The head was removed exposing the 4 cylinders, which John closely inspected with a flashlight. One of the cylinder sleeves was damaged, having heavy scratches. John pointed it out to Grant.

"I'll bet when we pull these pistons out, we'll find broken rings on this one."

"How can you tell?" Grant asked.

"Run your fingernail along the sleeve wall," John told him. Which Grant did until his nail fell into one of the grooves. "Feel that?"

"Yes." Grant replied.

"That's bad enough to allow oil to get past the rings. It explains why this old girl smoked so badly when I brought her home."

Next, John went to his tool box and removed a 3 foot long, ¼" thick, 3" wide, flat steel bar and a small pneumatic angle grinder. He peeled the old head gasket off the top of the block and cleaned both the top of the block and the bottom of the head with the die-grinder fitted with a bright-pad disc. Then, using the edge of the flat iron, he checked both the block and the head for flatness.

"What are you doing?" Grant asked.

"This tool is called a straight edge," John explained. "It is straight and true, within 1,000th of an inch. By running the straight edge over the mating surface of both the block and the head, I am checking to see if one or the other has to be milled. And we are lucky there, both are flat and true."

Next, they mounted the engine on an engine stand and before turning the engine over, John grabbed a box of Tide powered laundry detergent and sprinkled it all around the engine stand. Grant was curious but didn't ask why, choosing instead to simply watch. The answer was short in coming. The moment they turned the engine over, old oil and coolant leaked out through the headless top of the block.

John set the head up on the bench and showed Grant how to remove the valves and valve springs. While Grant took the head apart, John removed the oil pan, oil pump, rod and main caps. Before he pulled the caps, he used a flat chisel to mark them, and then a quick photo of the bottom of the rolling assembly clearly showing the chisel marks. He finally lifted the crank out of the block and then popped each of the four pistons out. Sure enough, the number three piston had two broken rings.

Before loading all the old parts into the back of the truck, John had Grant sit at the bench with pen and paper to make notes as John loaded the truck. It was clear that the rest of the day would probably be spent running around town getting parts here, and dropping off parts there. As they went from place to place, they talked, told stories and laughed. Finally, John got to the thing that had always been on his mind.

"Who were the three boys you punched?"

"Just some buttheads." Grant's facial expression instantly changed.

"Okay, then why did you punch those buttheads? I think I know you well enough to know there had to be a good reason."

"There was." Grant answered.

"And that was??"

"Doesn't matter now." Grant wasn't ready to talk about it, so John let it go.

When they finally got back to the garage, Debbie was waiting for them.

11

John pulled a prepackaged TV dinner from the freezer and carefully prepared it per the instructions and tossed it into the microwave. While he waited for it to cook, he thought about his progress in getting to really know and understand Grant. He had gained insight, certainly. He even saw traits in the boy that he truly admired. He also realized that he really enjoyed having Grant with him. What he lacked was an understanding of what made Grant, Grant. What were his true passions? How did he see his future? More importantly, why did he seem to lack a sense of responsibility? He didn't seem to care at all about complying with what was expected of him by his family or the world in general. He couldn't help but wonder what those other boys had said that tripped Grant's trigger.

He suddenly had an idea. He flipped his phone open and placed a call to an old schoolmate that he had kept in touch with throughout life. Joe had always been the type that could feel the vibes of those around him. John smiled at the word vibes. It was one of those words that had been way over-used in the late 60's and early 70's and now was hardly uttered by anyone. The most important reason John thought of Joe at the moment, was that Joe worked at the school Grant attended. The phone was answered on the third ring. "Hello?"

"Joe, John Liggett."

"Hey John, what's up?"

"You busy right now?" John asked.

"Just rolling the mop bucket from the boy's restroom to the girl's." Joe laughed. "Always do the easiest one first."

"Boy's restroom easier to clean than the girl's?" John asked with a surprised laugh.

"Oh my yes! A lot easier." Joe replied with a disgusted tone of voice. "Those little females are pigs I tell you. Pigs. You wouldn't believe half the stuff I've seen in their restrooms. In the boy's restroom, the biggest problem is poor aim, the stalls are usually not bad, but the girl's, well that's another matter."

"I would have never guessed." John laughed.

"What's on your mind, John? I am sure you didn't call to get the latest on the janitorial trade."

"Joe, do you know my grandson, Grant Crawford?"

"Of course, I know Grant. Good kid. Quiet and shy, and keeps to himself mostly, but a good kid."

"Really?" John hadn't heard anyone but himself, Jan, and the girls use the term "a good kid" when talking about Grant before. It was reassuring to hear someone outside of the family say it.

"Yes really." Joe replied, surprised that the boy's own grandfather doubted it. "You worked up over what happened the other morning?"

"Well, to be honest, yes I am," John answered. "Grant doesn't seem to want to talk about it, and I need to know what happened."

"The boy stood up for what's right, that's what he did."

"What do you mean?"

"Those little, spoiled brats he knocked on their tails had it coming."

"Why, what did they do to Grant?"

"Oh nothing to Grant, they don't have the courage to face someone like that boy of yours."

John sat silent for a moment, thinking.

"You still there, John?"

"Yeah, I am," John replied. "Maybe you better start at the top. Tell me the whole story."

"Well, I am not paid to be on this phone." Joe said. "I suppose I could give you the Reader's Digest version of events if that helps."

"Please."

When John closed the phone ending the call, he had gained a lot of insight into the character of his grandson. Joe had told him to be proud of the boy no less than a dozen times. Before the call ended, John asked Joe to look a little deeper into one aspect of the story. Joe promised he would, and was also able to supply the phone number and extension of the school's botany teacher.

John decided to eat his already almost cold food before calling the teacher and requesting help with the gardens. Joe had already supplied some interesting information that John hoped to act upon. He just needed to think his approach through. The moment he finished eating, he placed the call and carefully worded his message. He wanted to be sure to make the call before he forgot half of the things he had just thought of, and before he was struck with indigestion, that he was sure was coming from that food. Oh, how he missed Jan and her ability to make the plainest of foods taste incredible.

Right on time, Debbie arrived the following morning with Grant. Like her mother, she was a creature of habit. She kissed her father's cheek and then her son's and exited through the door while telling them to be good. Grant didn't even ask permission before reaching into the cupboard and grabbing his grandmother's favorite cup and filling it with sugar and cream and a dash of coffee to properly liquefy the concoction. They had nearly completed their to-do list when Grant asked about the first time John had driven a tractor.

"I rode with my dad and grandfather a lot before I was ever allowed to drive one," John replied. "The key word being allowed."

"Oh-oh," Grant laughed. "I hear a tale of a different kind than I am used to hearing about you."

"Like all kids," John laughed. "I had my moments."

"I'm listening." Grant urged him on.

"You have to understand that that old tractor out in the garage was at one time your great-grandfather's prized possession. He had saved up for it, and it was the first major purchase he had ever made. In fact, he bought it a

89

year before he married my mother. I was born just a year after they married, so the tractor was only a few years old, considered like new, by the standards of the time. Today, modern farmers rotate equipment at a much faster rate than back then. I was about five years old, and somehow I figured out how to start it. Luckily, I never was able to get it into gear but my dad heard the engine and came running into the shed and snatched me off that tractor so fast that I remember it as a blur."

"What did he do to you?"

"What all parents of the time did to children when they misbehaved. I got my bottom spanked, and spanked good."

"Really?"

"Yes, really." John could remember that spanking well. It was the maddest he had ever seen his father. He would later learn that it was the most frightened his father had ever been. "I thought he was just mad at me, but years later he told me it scared him to death. If I had been able to somehow get that tractor into gear, it would have likely smashed through the back wall of the shed, which probably would have killed me. It was years before he started leaving the key in the tractor again."

"Wow." Grant had never heard this story before.

"Anyway," John continued, just as his phone rang. He answered the phone, it was the parts store informing him that his engine kit, and Vickers hydraulic pump seal kit and the PTO shaft seal were in. John told them that they would pick them up that morning and hung up. He continued the story for several minutes before the phone went off again. This time, it was the sandblasters informing him that his parts had been blasted and were ready for pickup. He again said that they would be there that morning to get them. He had barely closed his phone when it rang again. This time, the machine shop was calling to say that the crank was ready. "It seems that God wants us to get back to work."

"So your dad and grandpa had you start riding on the tractors with them." Grant wanted the rest of the story.

"That very year I started riding on the tractors and both spent many hours teaching me to respect and fear machinery. The next year I began to sit on their laps and steer. Finally, I suppose I was eight at the time, my father actually gave me driving lessons. The first of which was how to back a wagon. He always told me that unless I could prove that I knew how to back a rig up, he wasn't going to trust me to drive it forward."

"Were you nervous?"

"I was nervous and excited at the same time," John explained. "It was that old tractor out in the garage."

"That's cool." Grant smiled.

"It always was a well-mannered tractor. What I mean by that is that it was easy to drive and handle. As I recall, the first try took a few minutes, but I got the wagon where my dad wanted it. We spent the balance of the day practicing the maneuver until I could do it almost as fast as my father could. By fall, I was driving on a regular basis."

"When you were eight?" Grant couldn't believe it.

"Those were different times." John looked at his grandson and weighed his thoughts on whether he should

91

say what he wanted to or hold back. He decided to say what he felt. "I took pride in the trust my parents and grandparents had in me to be responsible and safe. I also felt an obligation to fulfill that trust by doing what was expected of me, regardless of whether the task was large or small."

Grant didn't say anything, just looked into his grandfather's eyes. The message was delivered and received.

The next hour and a half was spent running from one place to another to pick up parts. Grant was beginning to see just how much this project was costing his grandfather. By 10, they were back at the garage and getting everything unloaded. Once everything was inside the garage and lying on the floor around the tractor's chassis, John had an idea.

"Grant, I have a project for you."

"Okay," Grant was eager to do something, hopefully important.

John led him over to where the hood, front and rear fenders, nose piece and grille were laying. "To properly fix and finish these parts, we need to design and build stands that will allow us to work on them, sand, and then paint them. It must be stable enough to not fall over while we are working on the part it holds, and yet must have as little contact with the part as possible so that we can paint the part as completely as possible."

"Okay," Grant said slowly. "What do you want me to do?"

"That's simple," John laughed. "Design those stands and remember we don't have a lot of room, and be thrifty. You can design them out of wood or steel, or both actually. We will only use them once, so I want you to keep the cost of material in mind as well."

"Whoa," Grant sighed. "Papa, I don't think I am up to that kind of challenge."

"I think you are." John was firm. "Unless you try, how would you know?"

Grant didn't reply, just looked into John's eyes, hoping that maybe he was kidding. He wasn't.

"Go into my office and get a couple of pencils, a ruler, and some paper. You'll find all of that in the right bottom drawer."

"You mean it?" Grant wasn't believing what he was being asked to do.

"Yes, of course," John replied. A motion of his finger toward the door told him to go. When Grant came back to the garage, John set him up at the workbench and gave him an idea of how to go about it. "Take the rear fenders as an example." Of course, John took the easiest of the parts to make an example of. "See how the fender braces are formed to allow them to be bolted to the axles?"

"Yeah," Grant was nervous, but intrigued.

"All we have to do is use that ease of installing design to our advantage." John walked to the back corner of the garage and found a four foot 2x8 plank. Then he went to the bolt/screw hanging rack on the other side of the garage and looked for and found four long screws and washers he wanted to use. He then laid the plank down next to the fenders and asked Grant to hold the first fender to the top of the plank, close to the left edge. He quickly inserted two of the screws with the washers using his cordless drill. When he was done with that fender, he had Grant hold the other fender at the other end of the plank and attached that in the same manner. When John stood up, the two fenders were standing upright on the plank.

"Now all we have to do is set that plank on a couple of sawhorses, and we're good to go."

John left Grant to his work and focused his attention on removing the hydraulic pump and cleaning both it and the engine block. In less than ten minutes, Grant was over at the back of the garage looking through the pile of scrap boards and steel John had been putting there for years. After sorting through the pile for a few minutes, Grant went back to the pieces of sheet metal lying on the floor and took a few measurements before returning to the work bench and his drawings. John was sure Grant would ask a number of questions about how to go about it, but not once did Grant say anything.

Ten more minutes went by with Grant busy at the bench before he got up with his drawings and went back to the scrap pile and started pulling items out and measuring them. When he had the collection of pieces he wanted, he went back to the shelf next to the workbench and looked through it until finding a coil of mechanic's wire and some twine. His next stop was at the bolt and screw bin. Finally, Grant went to work assembling his creation.

John stayed busy getting the parts for the engine laid out but also kept an eye on what Grant was constructing. When Grant had finished, John was both proud and amazed. Every piece of sheet metal was secured in the rack Grant had made using junk that had been lying around. Each piece of metal was attached using the least amount of contact points which would make painting the pieces easier and with less touch-up in the end. John stopped what he was doing and walked around the hand-made jig in silence. Grant watched his grandfather with baited breath.

When John finished walking around Grant's creation in silence, he looked up at his grandson in pure admiration. "Son that is the best painting jig I have ever seen. It fills all criteria to perfection. You are absolutely amazing when you set your mind to something." Grant was beaming from ear to ear.

"To show you just how well you've done," John said while stepping over to the tool box and retrieving a couple of hammers. "We'll put it to the test, which I think it will pass with flying colors."

John spent the next hour showing Grant how to do bodywork. They carefully slid their flat hands across the blasted metal not only looking for, but feeling for, any divots or dents. When one was found, John placed the bigger of the two hammers on the low side of the metal and tapped the high side with the smaller hammer until as little of the dent remained as possible. Next, he took a sander and sanded the metal looking for high spots. These he carefully dimpled slightly, explaining that it was better too low than too high, since they could fill the low spots.

Grant's stand did perfectly. It not only held the pieces so they could work on them, but held them securely. Once they had done as much with the hammers as possible, John showed Grant how to mix and apply body filler. He then had Grant finish filling the areas they had marked out in pencil, while he finished getting the engine ready to be built.

With all the panels now filled with filler, the sheet metal had to sit and allow the filler to cure. John had first planned on having Grant scrape and clean on the chassis while he rebuilt the engine. After seeing how well Grant had done with the stand, he decided that the boy wouldn't learn anything scraping, he already knew how to do that.

For the next three hours, they pulled the old sleeves out of the block and installed the new ones. They fitted the old pistons with the new rings and after coating them in assembly lube, fitted them into the new sleeves. John then showed Grant how to install the rod and main bearings and how to use a set of plasti-gauges to check bearing clearance. Satisfied all was as it should be, they coated everything in assembly lube, set the timing gears in the proper place, and torqued the rod and main caps to specs after fitting the front and rear main seals. The new oil pump and pickup were installed, followed by the oil pan and front timing cover.

They then turned the engine upright on the engine stand and finished assembly of the top end of the engine. They had just completed the task when Debbie came through the door and commented that she loved that smell, whatever it was.

"Assembly lube and bondo," John quipped. "The quickest way to a girl's heart."

Debbie laughed, and then commented that it looked like they had been busy.

96

"You don't know the half of it," John replied as he took her by the hand and led her over to the rack Grant had made. He then explained that none of it had existed that morning, and how he had tasked Grant with designing and building something that would fill their needs. He finished by saying; "That son of yours is absolutely brilliant when challenged and left to his own devices."

All the way home that night, Debbie couldn't stop talking about how proud she was of Grant. She had never seen her father so impressed as he was right now.

"Okay Mom, I did good. Thanks." Grant finally said to calm his mother down.

John finished picking up the tools and wiping them off before putting them away in the tool box. He kept glancing over at the stand and smiling. It had been a great day with Grant. The boy had really come through with that stand and surprised the dickens out of him. After the tools were all put away, he went into the house and took a shower before picking through the selection of frozen dinners he had picked up. Opting for the country fried steak, he popped it into the microwave just as his phone rang. It was his buddy Joe, with the information he had requested.

Halfway through his supper, the phone rang again. This time it was the biology teacher, who also taught the class on botany. She told him that she found his request a little unusual. John then proceeded to explain the whole story to her. About losing his wife recently and how the flower gardens had always been her passion and how he now saw those gardens as a living part of her. Evidently,

John had made a good case of it because by the time he finished the teacher was not only on board with the idea, but said that she would find the help John was looking for, or she would help him out herself.

John thanked her for that, but reiterated that he was hoping to find a student in need. Someone that could truly use the funds he was offering. He told the teacher that the student could bring their parents with them, but that the student had to know what they were doing and have a passion for it.

"I have just such a student in mind," The teacher replied. "I will talk to her tomorrow and call you back around this time if that is okay."

12

Just like clockwork, Debbie delivered Grant at the same time every morning, which was just fine with John. He wasn't as rigid in his routines as Jan had been, but he still liked things he could count on, and Debbie's punctuality was one such thing. John was already sitting at the table having coffee when they came through the door. True to form, Debbie kissed her father's cheek first and then her son's. At the door, she always spun on her heels and warned them to behave.

Grant was already fixing his coffee in Jan's cup when John spoke. "Do you ever notice how your mother does exactly the same thing, the same way, every morning."

"Oh, don't even get me started down that path, Papa." Grant shook his head. "I've heard you and Mom talk about how Grandma was with her routines. Well, let me tell you, her daughter is ten times worse."

"Really?" John was smiling at Grant's reaction.

"Papa, you have no idea. If things don't go as she has planned, look out!"

"Really? Have you ever said something to her about it?"

"Almost."

John looked at Grant a second. "Almost?"

"She doesn't think she has a problem," Grant replied. "One day she was scolding me for not putting my dirty clothes in the hamper. I told her that I didn't do it because I rarely do it. So rarely, in fact, that I figured that picking up my dirty clothes was part of her routine, and I sure didn't want to rock that boat."

John burst out laughing. "How did she respond to that logical answer?"

"It was weird," Grant replied. "She instantly stopped picking the clothes up and stood up and glared at me. I mean she literally froze in place for like ten or fifteen seconds. Then she just bent down and grabbed the last of my clothes and left. Not one word spoken."

John was laughing. "She is her mother's daughter. That sounds like the way your grandmother would have reacted."

"Freaked me out," Grant admitted.

"Did you have your clothes picked up the next time?"

"Oh yeah," Grant answered with a nod and wide eyes.

They spent the next ten minutes making out the to-do list for the day. This morning differed from the others in that Grant took an active role in the planning of their day. He was really getting the hang of breaking big jobs down into small ones. He was also learning how to visualize what had to happen and in what order. As they were leaving the house for the garage, John commented on Grant's ability to pick things up quickly and how much nicer it was to plan the day together.

"The 5 ps," Grant smiled back at him.

In the garage, they sanded all of the sheet metal parts and carefully inspected what they had before refilling

100

those parts that needed it. Once they had accomplished that task, they moved over to the vise on the edge of the workbench. There John carefully took the Vickers hydraulic pump apart. Each part was laid out on a clean paper towel in the order it came off the pump. Once everything was apart, John showed Grant what to look for. Together they inspected the seals and found two that had been leaking. Then they checked the bearings and the little metal vanes that drove the hydraulic fluid through the system. Once everything had been inspected and cleaned and John was convinced that the seal kit he had ordered was all the pump needed, they began to put it all back together.

"How do you know how to do stuff like this?" Grant was amazed at what his grandfather could do.

"I'm a genius. I told you that already." John quipped with a firm voice and straight face.

"No, seriously." Grant said. "You're not, nor have you ever been a mechanic. So really, how do you know how to do this stuff?"

John stopped putting the pump back together. Instead, he took all the pieces apart and laid them back out on the bench as they had been.

"What are you doing?" Grant asked, surprised that he was taking it apart again.

John looked at Grant and smiled. "To start with, I was born on a farm, and I say that with a sense of pride. Farmers are as resilient and self-sufficient as any walk of life there is. When you're a farmer, you learn a lot of things city folks don't. You learn about crops, plants, animals, equipment. You become a veterinarian, a mechanic, and a

101

botanist. Not always because you want to learn those things, but more often than not it is because you have to. Living out in the country means you can't always run to the store to get something. Sometimes there isn't time, say like when an animal is being born or has been injured. You have to act and act right then to save its life. Sometimes the reason is monetary, you just don't have the money to buy a new part, so you have to think outside the box and find a way to fix it with what you have on hand."

Grant nodded his head in understanding.

"Just like you did yesterday, building that stand," John said while pointing his thumb towards Grant's sheet metal stand.

"Okay, makes sense," Grant replied. "But why did you just take what you had put together back apart?"

"Because I am not going to reassemble this pump."

"Why, is it broken?" Grant asked.

"No, there is nothing wrong with this pump other than it needs to be reassembled. And to answer your question, the reason I took it back apart is so you could put it back together." John smiled at Grant.

"Me? I don't know how to do that."

"I didn't know either, the first time I did something like this," John reassured him. "The first time is the hardest. Now, come stand where I am. We'll switch places."

Once they had traded places at the bench, Grant acted like he didn't know where to begin.

"Look at the parts," John told him. "They are laid out in the order that they came apart. Next to the old seals are the new ones."

"What about all those little parts?" Grant was nervous.

John picked up the base of the pump and placed it in Grant's hand. "You start with part number one. Worry about the next part when you get to it."

John stood silently while his grandson slowly put the pump back together. After putting the first several pieces together, Grant would look at his grandfather to get that nod that said he had done it right. By the time they were closing the pump up with the top cap, Grant was no longer looking over for approval. He was simply putting the next part or seal in place and moving on to the next.

Once the pump was securely back in its place on the engine, they moved to the rear of the tractor. The PTO shaft was pulled and that seal replaced and reassembled. Then John handed Grant a dust respirator, a pair of goggles, some ear plugs, and a plastic jumpsuit.

"About to get nasty?" Grant smiled.

"It sure is," John replied while putting his gear on and helping Grant into his. "From now until your mother gets here, we have a date with 60-year-old dirt, paint, grease, and probably manure." Grant just looked at him without saying a word. John stepped over to the tool box and retrieved two 4.5" angle grinders with wire wheels fitted to them. "We have to get this chassis as close to bare metal as possible."

Grant nodded his understanding.

103

"Wear these as well," John said while handing a pair of heavy leather gloves to him. "Those wire wheels hurt when they make skin contact."

Again Grant nodded.

"Also, as the wheels wear down, they will begin to spit out the wire. It will stick in anything it hits like little missiles. That includes body parts like skin and or eyes. They will always spit a little wire, so just beware, but when they start throwing a lot of it, change the wheel."

Okay," Grant nodded.

They had barely started stripping the chassis when the air around them became thick with heavy particles. John stopped what he was doing and opened the overhead garage door and set a fan up to blow it out.

By the time Debbie appeared to pick Grant up, the paint and grime on the chassis was so thin the polished cast showed through. Grant was the first to notice his mother and motioned to John, who called it a day.

Once they were out of their safety gear and Grant was about to leave, John asked him if he was going to be there in the morning?

"No, I have to go to my dad's."

"Well, that's alright," John replied. "We had a good week and accomplished a lot."

"We sure did," Grant smiled at the sight, then a thought worried him. "You're not going to finish it this weekend are you?"

"This is our project, not mine, ours. I wouldn't even want to finish it without my right-hand man here with me."

That made Grant smile broadly as he left the garage and got into the car. Once Grant was out of earshot Debbie turned to her dad.

"Well, it's been a week, how is it going?"

John cupped his sweet daughter's face in his big, dirty hands. "Been one of the best weeks of my life, darling. I would have decked those kids myself for this chance to be with Grant."

"Dad! That's not what I meant. Are you making any progress in straightening him out?"

John thought a moment and then gave her a reassuring smile. "I can't promise you that Grant will be a new boy when he goes back to school the week after next, or the next month after that. I will promise you that in time, in his own time. This time, will be thought of as well spent." He then felt a tick in his left arm and took his hands off her face and rubbed the painful spot.

"You okay?"

"Oh sure, just sore from doing things I am not used to," John smiled at her.

She kissed his cheek and turned to leave. "You don't know how much your being there for me during this has meant."

"Oh, but I do," John smiled. "If it has meant a fraction to you of what this week has meant to me, I do."

Once Debbie and Grant had left, John went to work sweeping the dirt off the garage floor. It was surprising to think that all that dirt had been attached to a single tractor, let alone a smaller sized Ford. Just as he was scooping the first of many dustpan loads of dirt, his phone chirped. "Hello?"

"Hello, Mr. Liggett?" The soft female voice asked.

"Yes, this is John Liggett."

"Mr. Liggett, this is Emily Roberts, a student at Fillmore High."

"Oh, yes."

"My teacher said you were looking for someone to teach you how to care for some flowers."

"Indeed, I am," John replied. "She told me that she had a gifted student that might be of some help. I'll pay you for your trouble."

The line was silent for a few seconds. "I would like to see what you have in mind first," Emily said.

"I think that would be a great idea." John agreed. "I think it would also be best if I were to meet your parents."

"My parents?"

"I know it sounds strange, I think it best in this day and age for you and me both to be safe. At least for the first meeting."

"Oh, okay." Emily didn't seem to mind that idea. "My dad said that he could bring me over, would that be all right?"

"Right now?" John asked.

"Yeah, if that's okay."

"Now would be fine," John replied. "Here is the address."

After she had the address, she said that they would be there in about half an hour, which would give John time to finish cleaning the garage floor.

13

When John closed his phone he had to smile. Everything had thus far gone to plan. He wasn't trying to play match-maker, Grant and this Emily were too young for that. What he really wanted was a glimpse inside his grandson's head. This girl, Emily Roberts, was someone Grant felt was worth standing up for and John couldn't wait to meet her. If he played his cards right, Grant would never know that he had met Emily. That was the reason for having her come over after Grant had left. It would probably only take two or three visits for him to learn how to care for the gardens, and he should be able to pull it off without Grant ever knowing a thing about it.

He had finished sweeping as much of the dirt off the floor as possible, but the floor still was covered in a fine powder, so John opened the big overhead garage door and connected the air hose. Starting at the back of the garage and blowing toward the door, he proceeded to blow the fine dust out of the garage. He was in the process of coiling the hose back up when the old car of the man that had borrowed the 9/16 flex-head socket during the garage sale, pulled into the drive. "Wonder what he wants?" John asked himself as he finished with the airhose and then stepped to the front of the garage. The man and one of his daughters got out of the car and walked toward him. It suddenly dawned on John that the girl just might be Emily Roberts.

"Working on the Jubie?" The man was all smiles as he stepped up to John and offered his hand.

"Yes," John smiled and took the man's hand. "Grandson and I decided to do the restoration together."

"Great father-son type project." The man said. "Looks like you've gotten a lot done." The man stepped past John and over to the chassis and the engine. "Engine all rebuilt?"

"It is," John replied. "Hydraulic pump rebuilt, new PTO seal, just have the rear axle seals and brakes to go. Well, that and finish stripping the old paint off."

"I'd say you're about ready for primer."

"Getting close," John agreed, then turned his attention to the young lady that had finally just stepped into the garage proper. "Are you Emily Roberts, my flower expert?"

The girl shyly nodded and turned to face John.

John held out his hand. "Emily, I'm John Liggett. Thanks for coming to look my gardens over. It means a great deal to me."

"You're welcome," Emily spoke softly and offered a slight smile that didn't reveal any teeth.

Mr. Roberts stepped back to where John and Emily were standing. "John, I'm Jim Roberts. We never actually exchanged names when you loaned me the tools. On the way home that day I thought about that, and was surprised you didn't even ask my name."

"I didn't even think about that," John confessed. "It was just a tool, and you struck me as an honest man."

"Thank you," Jim smiled. "That's a really clever stand you built for the sheet metal."

"It works out very well," John replied. "But I didn't build it, my grandson did. I just told him what we needed and he designed and built it himself using the material we had on hand."

"Clever boy, he'll go far in this world." Jim nodded toward the rack.

"I'm learning that more and more with each hour we spend together." John agreed before turning to Emily. "I don't want to take up your entire evening, so shall we take a look at the gardens?"

"Sure," Emily nodded and turned sideways in a gesture for John to lead the way. Emily and her dad followed John out of the garage and into the backyard where Jan had three distinctly different styled, but beautiful flower gardens. All bordered with stones, and two had cobblestone walks passing through them to allow access to the interior.

Emily went down on her knees at the first garden and felt the soil. She carefully examined the types of plants that the garden had. Then she moved to the second and finally the third, doing the same thing at each. The two men just watched her in silence until she stood up to face them. "These gardens are absolutely beautiful."

"No thanks to me," John admitted. "Jan planted them, cared for them, watered and weeded them. I just enjoyed them and watching her."

"I'm not sure what you're concern is," Emily stated.

"My concern," John thought his answer over. "Is that they are what they are because Jan spent a good deal of time making them that way and nurturing them. I, on the

110

other hand, know nothing about caring for flowers and to be honest, I am worried that without learning how to care for them, I will probably end up killing them."

"They are a lot hardier than you think," Emily replied. "What are your main concerns?"

"My main concern is this. I see these gardens as a living testament to my wife. I want… no, I need them to flourish. I need that part of her to continue to thrive. When I look at her gardens, I see her. I feel her presence when I am near these gardens."

Emily smiled a sad but understanding smile.

"I haven't a clue as to how to weed them, or how much or when to water them," John said.

"Watering them is pretty straight forward," Emily replied. "If we haven't had rain for a few days, water them."

"How much?"

Emily glanced up at John with an expression that said she was just beginning to understand just how little he really knew about plants. "Your soil will tell you how much."

"How so?"

"When you're watering, watch the soil," Emily instructed. "You water it until it looks well saturated but not flooded. It will begin to puddle when it has enough. During a cool but dry period, water every other day. During a hot, dry period, water every day."

"Okay, what about weeding?" John asked.

111

Emily almost smiled at that question. "When you see a weed, pull it. Other than that, once a month should suffice."

"Just how would I recognize what is and what isn't a weed?"

"Seriously?" Emily responded and John could see in her eyes, his stock just went down.

"Yes, I don't know one plant from another," John admitted. "I understand mechanical things. As you can see, I know how to restore a tractor. I can wire a house, fix a car, manage a retail store, back a trailer and so many other fine manly things, but I haven't a clue when it comes to detecting a weed amongst flowers. Unless, of course, the flowers are in bloom, and that's not always the case."

"True," Emily nodded and turned to the garden closest to where they stood. She carefully looked the garden over until she found what she was looking for and knelt down beside it. She reached out and pulled the tiny plant from the soil and placed it in her palm and offered her palm up so John could see it. "This is a weed."

John grabbed his phone out of his pocket and hit the picture button and quickly snapped a picture of it. As soon as he had the picture he looked at Emily, whose eyes were wide in amazement. "Just so I can recognize it when you're not here," John confessed.

"Really? ... Oookay." Emily nearly laughed at that. "You're lucky in that your wife kept the weeds down very well. If you look, the weeds, what few there are, are just breaking the soil and are in their infancy."

112

After Emily went through each garden showing John what to look for, she promised that next time she came out, she would try to borrow the school's soil tester. She then proceeded to dead-head the flowers, which meant removing the old blooms. While she worked, John and Jim talked. During the conversation, John learned that Jim was a carpenter and had just started his own remodeling business. He was enjoying it, but at the moment work was slow. John instantly thought of several friends and said he would put the word out for him.

Before they left, John paid Emily for her time. She tried to refuse the money, but John insisted. They set an appointment for the following Friday night about the same time for her to come back and test the soil and give him another lesson in weeds.

14

John popped another frozen dinner into the microwave and thought about life not being what he had planned. If Jan was here, he would be about to enjoy something really tasty. Instead, he was about to eat some very processed piece of meat, and while doing so, wonder if whatever it was had ever really lived. The corn and the chocolate dessert were both good, but the dessert was about the size of a postage stamp. He had just finished eating and was washing the silverware in the sink when his phone chirped. He pulled it from his pocket and checked the number before answering. It was his old friend Burt Herrington.

"Hey, uglier than me," John said the moment he answered the call.

Burt laughed out loud. "Well, that would be ugly indeed."

"What are you up to, Burt?"

"I went by your place the other day. Stopped and couldn't find you anywhere around, but I noticed something in your yard beside the garage." Burt said.

"The boat?"

"The boat," Burt confirmed. "When did you get a boat?"

"A week ago."

"Had it out yet?" Burt asked.

"Took it out last weekend with Debbie and her family," John replied. "Had a great time."

"Got any plans this weekend?"

"Not really," John replied. "Thinking you might want to do a little fishing?"

"Well," Burt laughed. "Had lunch with Pete, Dan, and Rick this afternoon. One of them asked about you, and I told them about stopping by your place and finding the boat."

"And a plan was hatched," John smiled.

"You furnish the boat," Burt went into the plan. "We furnish the food, beer, and bait."

"How could I turn down an offer like that?" John laughed. "Where do you want to meet up and when?"

"Tomorrow morning at Sam's place for breakfast, say around 7."

"You're on. See you at Sam's at 7." John agreed, glad to have something to do that weekend.

John was up at 5, turned the coffee pot on and headed for the shower. After enjoying that first cup of coffee, he slipped a light jacket on, went out and uncovered the boat and hooked the trailer to the back of the truck. It took a little maneuvering to get it out of the side yard and into the driveway, but he had it ready well before time to leave for the restaurant. He had another cup of coffee and then rinsed the cup out in the sink. He had decided to fuel the boat up before meeting for breakfast, which should put him at the restaurant at the perfect time.

115

The gas station had six pumps and only four customers when John pulled in with the boat in tow. Amazingly, the four customers ahead of him had found a way to effectively block all six pumps. When they had filled their car's fuel tank, they left it blocking the pumps and took their time inside paying and getting coffee or rolls or whatever. By the time John was finally able to fuel the boat up and head to the restaurant, he was running late.

The guys were already in the restaurant enjoying coffee when John walked in. The pretty, young waitress asked if he wanted coffee, and had it to his spot at the table by the time he had his jacket off and sat down. It had been over a year since these men had all been together for breakfast. They had all been together at Jan's funeral, but today was going to be a day of fun and fellowship. Burt Herrington, a small framed man with flowing white hair, rosy complexion and an infectious laugh was a semi-retired dentist with a passion for fishing. Pete Sanderson was the opposite of Burt. He was a very large, heavy set man that had just retired from 40 years of driving semi-truck. Everything about Pete was large. From his six foot height, his 265-pound frame, to his meaty hands and fingers. Pete was far quieter than Burt, listening and thinking of what the others said. When he did speak, people listened. Just like his big frame, Pete had a big mind and could offer a good opinion on most topics.

The fourth man at the table was Dan Matting. Dan was always well-groomed and dressed. That morning he looked more like he was headed for a round of golf than a day fishing in the river. Dan was also a quick wit and always had great stories to make others laugh. Dan was over six foot and very fit. He spoke with an almost perfect modulated voice and was well known in town as the best

116

trial lawyer money could buy. The fifth man was Rick Lutz, a retired machinist. Rick was the shortest man in the group at five foot four inches tall and medium build. Rick was a strong supporter of trade unions, and a born and bred Democrat. He wore his light brown hair in a crew cut, and this morning was being kidded about his having it colored to prevent the natural graying the others displayed.

"Give Rick a break," John told those around the table. "I like his hair that way. He looks just like he did when I met him thirty years ago. Looking at him unchanged after all these years makes me feel younger."

The others laughed about that but had to agree.

After eating, they all followed John out to River Park. Each man had, at least, a case of beer and a cooler filled with sandwiches, fruit and iced tea. The tea was mainly for John, as he wasn't much of a beer drinker. It touched John that every one of his friends had brought his favorite brand of iced lemon tea for him. The boat was loaded and then launched. The morning air on the river was fresh and cool. The sun was climbing in the sky and would soon warm things up. They motored several miles up the river until Pete said that he always had good luck at a spot just ahead.

John brought the boat into Pete's lucky area slowly and maneuvered so the anchors could be set, and within minutes, there were 10 poles in the water. The first strike happened quickly and for the next three hours, the men had the time of their life catching and releasing, laughing and joking. Most of what they caught were carp, but Dan landed a largemouth bass, and Pete hooked a pike. After a picture was taken with the victorious angler, the fish were released. By noon, the men were getting hungry, and the fishing had slowed to an occasional bite now and then. They pulled the anchors and John motored over to an area that was protected from the sun by huge trees that grew out over the river.

The one thing that drew these men together as friends was their faith. As soon as the boat was snug against her anchors, the men stood, formed a circle and joined hands. Burt started the prayer by giving thanks for the opportunity to join together for a relaxing day on the river. Each man, in turn, added to the prayer until it came to John, the final man to pray. John also gave thanks, thanks for his friends, and thanks for the opportunity God had granted him with his grandson. Then John prayed for a family in need. Prayed for Jim Roberts to find work so he would be able to turn around the hard times that had befallen his family and be able to supply the basics for his family. Basics that most people took for granted.

The moment the prayer was over, the other men began questioning John about this family in need. John told of what he witnessed at the garage sale, the girls needing glasses and dental work. They could only afford a dollar each for much-needed clothing, and paid in quarters. Then about loaning Jim a tool to fix his battered and dying old car. He told of how Jim had brought the tool back so quickly. How the Roberts family had lost their farm and so on. He also told of learning that the kids at school were merciless in teasing the girls because of their poor teeth, broken glasses, and old clothing. Calling them names like Dragon Mouth, Goodwill Queen, and so forth. He also explained that his grandson, Grant, had been expelled not once, but twice, for standing up for one of the girls.

118

"How can we help?" Pete wanted to get to the heart of the matter.

"Well," John smiled, his friends had taken the bait. "The family has pride and won't readily accept charity. But Jim is a carpenter, just in need of work."

"Is he good?" Dan asked.

"No clue," John admitted. "But like I said before, he is honest. And that is paramount in a man's character."

"My wife has been wanting a new kitchen for years," Burt said while thinking of a different approach. "You say the girls need dental work?"

"They do."

"Think he might be open to a partial barter?" Burt asked.

"Maybe," John answered pensively. "The problem there would be in how to go about it. You can't just say that I told you the girl needed her teeth fixed. They might not appreciate our intentions."

"I see." Burt rubbed his chin.

"I can tell you that the girl has a passion for flowers and gardens. I needed help in caring for Jan's gardens and the oldest daughter, Emily, is who the teacher recommended. I called and she and her father came right over. She is really smart and helped me understand what I need to do to keep Jan's gardens flourishing."

Burt looked up at John with a sly smile. "The wife has always loved Jan's gardens and wanted us to do one, but neither of us really understand gardening. Maybe I can make the wife happy and hire both the dad and Emily."

Before they finished their lunch, all four of John's boat guests had thought of projects they could call Jim to do. The rest of the afternoon was spent just cruising the river as the fish had quit biting. After loading the boat, the men had one last prayer and gave thanks for a great time of fellowship and the opportunity to help others.

John was watering the gardens as Emily had instructed him when his phone chirped in his pocket. It was Jim Roberts calling to thank him for the referrals and promising not to let him down. He was also excited that one fellow even wanted to hire Emily to build a flower garden similar to the ones Jan had made.

15

John had the coffee made and laid out the notebook so he and Grant could plan their day. They had done well on the tractor last week, and he felt confident that they could complete it by Friday. That thought made him realize that he had just five more days of what he had come to think of as real quality time with his grandson. Last week went by so quickly, he was sure that this week would pass even faster.

Right on time, Debbie came through the side door with Grant in tow. Grant looked like he wasn't fully awake yet. Debbie came over and kissed her father's cheek and asked if he was okay. "Never better," He replied. She then kissed her son's cheek and headed for the door, stopping at the threshold and turning to remind them to be good.

"She must think you're a bad influence," Grant said once his mother was out the door.

"Me?" John looked at Grant as the boy reached into the cupboard and pulled Jan's cup out. "Maybe she knows I am easily influenced and doesn't want me to be led astray by you."

Grant laughed at that idea as he made the syrupy concoction he called coffee. John pointed out that this was their last week to finish their project.

"We're close," Grant replied. "We'll have it done probably by Wednesday."

"Well, we are close, but not as close as you think." John corrected him.

Before making the to-do list for that day, John wanted to do a detailed item list for the project. The intent was to break down what had to be done, from where they were, to the finished job. Grant was surprised by the sheer number of items on that list. When they felt that they had listed each and every task before them, that list was broken down into five segments. One for each day left to complete the restoration. As John looked the list over, he put a star next to several of the items on the list.

"Why did you do that?" Grant wanted to know.

"These are items that may have to be done out of sequence, in order to be ready when the time comes. Case in point," John said pointing to an item on the list. "We need to have new tires and tubes installed onto the rims, so that when the tractor is ready, we can install them. For the tires to get mounted, we have to prepare the rims now. Which means getting them in paint today, so they can cure overnight, then take them to the tire dealer tomorrow. I will call them today to be sure they have the tires in stock. If they don't, they can get them ordered today."

The to-do list was based on what they had to accomplish that day to stay on course. They finished their coffee and went out to the garage to get started. First order of business was to sand the sheet metal and do one last fill with body filler. Next, they gathered the front wheels and rear rims that the sandblaster had stripped for them. John showed Grant how to properly hand sand them to make sure they were ready for primer. While Grant was doing that, John set about removing the rear brake drums and brake parts. Then he pulled the axles and bearings for inspection.

By this time Grant had the wheels and rims ready for primer, so John cleaned his hands and showed Grant how to mix the three part primer. John sprayed the two rear rims while Grant watched how he did it. Then John handed the gun to him and had him spray the front wheels. For a first time, the boy seemed a natural. They set the freshly primed rims and wheels outside in the shade of the garage's over-hang. With nothing else to be primed that day, John showed Grant how to clean out a paint gun and set it for storage.

They then moved to the rear axle on the chassis. They had to replace the axle seals while being careful to install the right number of shims and put silicone between each shim. Then they needed to rebuild the brakes and put the drums on. When all of that was complete, they could turn their attention to finishing the stripping of the chassis itself. While they worked, Grant asked why John had left the farm and moved to town.

John explained that he had a younger brother that dearly loved farming. "From the time Richard could walk, he wanted to be a farmer. I guess I always knew it meant more to him than me, so I just felt letting him have the farm was the right thing to do. Besides, he would have to share the farm with our parents until such time as they either retired or died. You see, that is the way a lot of farming families work handing the farm down to the next generation. It was how my parents got it from their parents and so on."

"You weren't into sharing?" Grant teased.

"Actually, you are sort-of right," John smiled at him. "One can make a good living on the farm. Two can make a decent living, but three families trying to live off one farm, gets pretty tight."

"I bet." Grant nodded his head.

"Anyway," John continued. "I realized that there just wouldn't be enough to go around if I wanted to stay, and my parents seemed relieved when I said that I wanted to move to town when your grandmother and I got married. Then about five years later, my parents decided to retire after Dad had a heart attack. True to the way my parents thought things through, Richard was given a third of the land as his inheritance. An amount equal to the value of that gift was set aside for me. Richard was to make bi-yearly payments to them to pay off the farm and finance their retirement. Since my parents didn't really have enough money to set aside to cover my share, they set it up so that part of each land payment they got from Richard went into my account."

"Bet that added up in a hurry," Grant said.

"It wasn't as much as you might think, because land wasn't so high back then. But for the time, it was a sizable amount." John explained. The first four years or so went very well for Richard. He actually bought a smaller farm that was right behind our homestead. And he got a deal on it. The bank rolled both farms into one note and Richard was able to pay Mom and Dad off and settled my account."

"Bet that made you happy."

"Yes," John agreed. "I was happy for all of us. I was glad to see Richard doing so well, and relieved that Mom and Dad could live comfortably. Your grandmother and I bought this house with that money. Everybody got what they wanted."

"Why didn't you go back to the farm when Richard died?" Grant asked.

"It wasn't as easy as that. About two years after Richard bought that other farm the bottom fell out of crop prices. Then draught conditions, and having over-extended himself, left the farm deep in debt."

"What exactly happened to him?" Grant asked.

"He had gotten the bank to give him one more season," John explained. "Crop prices were looking better, and he sold about a third of what he expected to harvest on futures."

"What are futures?"

"It's a contract between a farmer and a co-op or another grain dealer. It offers a guaranteed price for a guaranteed amount of grain. The up-side of the futures is that it guarantees a price that the farmer can live with, and guarantees a product for the dealer when the time comes. The down-side is that if the crops don't come in and the price for that crop is higher than what the contract pays, the farmer must then buy grain on the open market to fill his contract."

"That's why he only sold a third of his expected production on futures," Grant figured it out.

"Right, to be sure he could fill the contract."

"So how did that lead to his death?" Grant asked.

"Well, he wanted the best crop he could get, and to do so, he plowed every inch of ground he could, including ground too close to the river. The bank gave away under the weight of the tractor and he tipped over into the river."

"Oh wow, I am sorry Papa."

"Thank you," John smiled at Grant. "The sad part was that his wife had already left him when the money had gotten real tight, so no one missed him when he didn't come home that night."

"How did they find him?"

"Well, your great-grandparents had tried calling that day, and again that night," John explained. "It was before cell phones, so a lot of calls went unanswered, but answering machines were new and Richard had one. When he didn't call back by the next morning, Mom and Dad drove out to the farm and looked for him. Dad couldn't get around very well by then, so Mom did most of the looking, and it was she who found the overturned tractor. She tried to get into the crushed tractor cab, but couldn't. Luckily, the water was very muddy and she couldn't see much, but she had seen a boot and knew he was in there. She ran all the way back to the farmhouse and called the Sheriff. The Sheriff had a wrecker come out and pull the tractor out of the river and Richard was found inside. Luckily, he had been crushed and probably died instantly. At least, I like to think he did."

"Beats drowning, I suppose." Grant agreed.

"Richard wasn't the only farmer in trouble that year," John remembered back. "A cousin was also in financial trouble, and like Richard, the stress led to marital troubles. When it became too much, he walked into the bank and shot the manager."

"Really?"

"Yeah, really," John replied. "He was a gentle, kind man all of his life. Always the first person to offer help when others were in need. None of that matters now; all people remember is that he is a killer and that he'll never get out of prison."

"Wow." Grant shook his head.

"The moral of the story, Son, is that every day we write another page into the story of our lives. Live your life so that every day the pages get better and better. When we're gone and people remember us, it is the sum total of those pages that defines us as human beings."

"I like that analogy." Grant smiled. "Believe it or not, I do try to do what I see as being right."

John winked at him. He had already learned that his grandson did indeed stand up for what was right, especially when it came to protecting others, but he wasn't going to show his hand. "I'm very glad to hear that Grant. And the more I get to really know you, the more I would expect no less."

When John felt that they had cleaned the chassis as much as they could, he glanced up at the clock and realized that they had just enough time to get the wheels, rear hubs and rims painted. John had Grant bring them in as he got the paint supplies out and set up on the bench. After setting the wheels and rims up on make-shift stands, John showed Grant how to mix the paint by adding reducer and hardener.

The larger rear rims were painted silver first and moved to the back of the garage. Then after cleaning the gun out, Ford medium gray or 8N gray as it was better known, was mixed.

"That doesn't look gray," Grant commented as he watched John mixing the paint. "Think they gave us the wrong paint? That is more light green."

John laughed. "First thing everyone says when they see this paint, but it is the right stuff. A unique color Ford called medium dark gray.

Debbie walked into the garage just as John was finishing cleaning the gun. The over-spray wasn't great, but she instantly started motioning for Grant to get out of the garage. When John finally stepped out of the garage and removed his respirator, Debbie stepped up in front of him.

"Dad, I don't think Grant should be in there while you're painting."

"What? Why?" John was surprised by her apparent agitation.

"Those fumes are bad for you." Debbie quickly said. "I know I can't stop you from doing what you want, but I don't want my son exposed to that."

"For heaven's sake little girl, calm down." John shook his head. "Didn't you notice that he was wearing a respirator just like mine? I wouldn't expose him unprotected to something that could hurt him."

"I saw him just standing there watching you paint."

"And your point?" John asked.

"The point is that he didn't need to be in there, he wasn't doing anything but watching you." Debbie countered.

"If he doesn't watch, how will he learn?"

Debbie looked into her father's eyes. He had a point, but there was one tiny little flaw in his theory. "And just how many old tractors do you think Grant will paint once he learns how?"

John laughed at that. "Maybe none, maybe 150, but who knows. Learning how to mix and spray paint is not just for painting tractors, but for painting anything. He might decide he likes painting and go on to be a successful body man at some body shop. Learning any task is not just about the task at hand, but about learning how to accomplish any task before you."

Debbie didn't reply, just looked at her father.

John stepped closer to her and bent down to look her in the eyes. "Baby girl, we already know that Grant is never going to be a Rhoades Scholar. The best thing we can do for him is to expose him to a variety of different jobs and who knows, he might just latch on to one of them."

16

John grabbed his first cup of coffee for the day and sat down to think what absolutely needed to happen that day to meet their goal of completion by Friday night. He was looking over their master list when Debbie came through the side door with Grant right behind. Grant appeared to be wide-eyed and alert and ready for the day. While his mother came over to her father's side and asked him how he was, Grant reached into the cupboard and retrieved Grandma's favorite cup, now his favorite. Debbie kissed John's cheek, then stepped over to Grant who was stirring his coffee and kissed his cheek. Just before stepping out the door, she turned toward the men. Both stopped what they were doing and looked at her expectantly.

"You two behave today, okay?"

John and Grant looked at each other and smiled.

"What?" Debbie demanded to know what they found so funny.

"We love you too little girl," John replied with a fatherly smile.

Debbie looked at her father and son, but not really buying what they seemed to be selling. "Just be good."

Once Debbie had left, Grant settled at the table next to John, "I don't think she trusts you, Papa."

"Me?" John looked at Grant. "I think she is afraid you will corrupt me."

"Yeah, right."

The first thing they had to do was get the freshly painted rims and wheels down to the tire dealer. On the way there, John said a prayer that the tires would be in. As they pulled into the parking space next to the store, they spotted a semi-truck unloading tires, and just as they got out of the truck they spotted two front tractor tires come off the truck. John turned around and glanced at Grant, who smiled back and nodded his head. When John turned his attention back to the semi's trailer, the first of two 12.4 x 28 Firestone rear tractors tires were being unloaded.

"Boy, we timed that perfectly," Grant said.

"The power of prayer, Son. The power of prayer." John said as he stepped to the back of his pickup and lowered the tailgate. "Let's get these rims and wheels inside."

Once everything inside, John paid for the new tires, tubes and mounting. A bill that made Grant's eye go wide, but he didn't say what he thought until they were safely back in John's truck.

"$1,850 bucks?!" Grant was stunned by the price.

"Yes, tractor tires are not cheap," John replied. "I suppose I could have gotten some cheap Chinese tires, but I wanted what was on it originally. Well, at least, what was on it when I drove it as a kid."

"So what's next?" Grant asked.

"Well," John pondered that question a moment. "The man said that we could pick the tires up in a couple of hours. I say we make a run to the parts store. We need a 12-volt battery, new wiring, lights, and electrical connectors."

131

"Let's 'git 'er' done!'" Grant did his best impression of Larry the Cable Guy. Which made John laugh.

Just as they were loading the parts they picked up at the parts store, John's phone chirped. It was the tire store informing him that the tires wouldn't be ready until later that afternoon. "Well, that isn't what we planned, so we might as well head home. Hopefully, the parts ordered from Steiner's Tractor Parts® will be there when we get home."

"Why don't you just pray for that?" Grant teased.

John looked over at his grandson, smiled and pulled the truck to the curb.

"What are you doing?" Grant asked.

"Following your suggestion of course, but I need your help."

"My help?"

"Yes," John said as he put the truck in park and turned toward Grant. "Give me your hands."

Grant reached out and allowed his grandfather to take his hands in his. "Father, we need these parts to be here so we can meet our goal of completing this project on time. More importantly, Father, I need my grandson to see your power to answer prayer. In the name of Jesus Christ, Amen."

John released Grant's hands and put the truck back into gear and drove home. Grant was quiet, not knowing what to make of what his papa had just done. He had never prayed before, wasn't sure if he even believed in God. His

132

mother always prayed, his father never did. When his mother prayed, it was always quietly, and personal, not meant for him to share in. At least, that is how he always felt.

When they pulled into the driveway, they both noticed the four boxes sitting at the front door. Grant looked over at John, and John returned his gaze with a sly smile.

"You ran tracking on them, didn't you?" Grant suddenly figured out what his papa had done.

"Actually, I meant to last night." John admitted, "However, 'the 'Note Book' was on the television. It was always your grandmother's favorite movie. Got lost in it, and simply forgot."

"Sure." Grant wasn't buying it.

"I swear to God," John replied.

Grant just looked at him and shrugged. Grant's mother had always said that if she wanted to know if something her father told her was true, she would make him swear it to God. If he did that, she knew it was true.

Once they had parked, they gathered up the boxes and carried them and the supplies they had just bought into the garage. They spread them out on the bench and went through them. The boxes from Steiner's included a 12-volt conversion kit with all the correct brackets to mount the General Motors one-wire alternator. Another box contained the new gauge kit, the next was the new seat pad and finally the small box containing a complete set of decals which included the red Ford script for the front and rear fenders.

133

"I'm amazed you can still get this stuff." Grant said while looking through the decals. He took the script decals and walked over to the sheet metal and compared the decals to the raised script lettering in the metal.

John followed him over. "To tell the truth, I would much rather have that script hand painted."

"Then why don't you?" Grant asked.

"Is your hand steady enough to do it?"

"No."

"Neither is mine." John shrugged. "We better get to work, or this day will be over and we will have accomplished nothing on our list."

"We dropped the wheels off, picked up the parts, and received the parts from Steiner's." Grant defended their efforts so far that day.

"True, but we have much more to accomplish, and hopefully, much of it before noon."

"Let's do it. "Grant laughed.

The first thing they did was hand sand the sheet metal and get it ready for another coat of primer. Then they washed the chassis down with thinner and blew it dry. John had Grant mix the 3 part primer, and the boy did an excellent job of it. Since he had done such a good job of mixing the primer, John had him do the spraying while he coached him along.

By noon, all the priming had been done and the gun cleaned out.

134

"Now what?" Grant asked as they stepped out of the garage.

"Well," John thought about it a moment. "We need to let that primer on the chassis flash before we can start painting. I say let's go for lunch."

"Sounds like a plan," Grant laughed. "I'm hungry. And maybe if you pray, the tires and wheels will be ready to pick up before we come home."

"Already took care of that," John smiled.

John took Grant to Sam's Place for lunch. The moment they walked through the door, John spotted Burt Herrington sitting by himself at a table. The moment Burt spotted them, he waved for them to come over and join him. "Hey, I called that carpenter you suggested." Burt blurted out as they neared the table. John shook his head to signal Burt to shut up. Luckily, Burt caught the signal and left it at that. John introduced Grant as they took a place at the table.

"You boys are lucky," Burt beamed. "I just got here myself and haven't ordered yet."

"Good thing," John agreed. "Otherwise, we would have to sit here and watch you eat."

"No point in letting food get cold." Burt laughed as the waitress came up and took their orders.

When the food came, Burt, John and Grant joined hands and took turns praying. It made Grant a bit uncomfortable, but he did say thanks for the time with his papa, and for the hands that prepared the food. When they closed the prayer, John looked over at Grant. "Son, you did well."

"First time in the water?" Burt asked with a smile.

"What?" Grant asked, confused.

"First time talking to God?" Burt answered. "The water bit is just an analogy for the realm of faith. It is that faith in Jesus Christ that cleanses us from sin, just as water washes the dirt from us."

Grant just nodded that he understood. The meal was pleasant as John and Burt chatted and made light fun of each other, which Grant seemed to enjoy. Burt even sprang for their lunch, which John argued about, but finally settled to accept so long as he could leave the tip.

Just as they were leaving the restaurant, John's phone chirped. It was the tire place telling him that his tires were ready to pick up. John snapped the phone shut and glanced over at Grant, who was smiling.

"The power of prayer," Grant laughed. "I know."

As soon as they got home, they unloaded the tires and wheels and stored them outside the garage so they wouldn't get red paint on them. The primer had flashed long enough. It was time to get the chassis painted. John explained what he wanted while Grant mixed the paint under John's supervision. The first coat was a very light coating that didn't cover well, but it would serve as a base for the other heavier coats. After the first light coat, they stepped outside to wait for the 1st coat to flash. Grant asked him what he meant when he said flash. John explained to

136

Grant that it was when the reducer used to thin the paint evaporated, and the surface seems to flatten out. This allowed the next coat to adhere to it. Since the reducer, the chemical that thinned the paint allowing it to be sprayed, from the first coat had evaporated, and that first coat had started to harden. Hopefully, the second coat would not run. To pass that time, John had Grant help him mount the painted rear hubs into the center of the rear rims.

The second coat was sprayed on heavier, but the paint itself was thinner. It took Grant about twenty minutes to coat the entire chassis. This time when they went outside to let the fresh paint flash, they sat under the maple tree and enjoyed some ice cold tea. Thirty minutes later they were back at painting. This third and final coat was even thinner than either of the first two and gave the chassis a shiny finish. John cautioned Grant to keep the gun moving. If he didn't, the fresh, thin, wet paint would puddle and run. Grant nodded and kept working. The final coat took less than twenty minutes to spray, then another five minutes for Grant to clean out the gun and seal all their supplies up.

Neither of them had seen Debbie step into the garage for a second before quickly retreating because of the overspray mist hanging in the air. When John and Grant emerged from the garage, she was standing just outside with her arms crossed. It wasn't until the men had washed up in the house that they got a good look at each other. Both had red hair, Ford Red hair.

"How is he going to get that red out of his hair?" She demanded when the men came out of the bathroom.

"What? You don't think he looks great with red hair?" John countered.

"Dad! His hair is full of paint." Debbie complained.

"But, it is tractor paint." Grant replied with a smirk directed toward his grandfather.

John caught the reference and smiled, but Debbie wasn't smiling. "If it doesn't wash out, it will wear off eventually."

"Dad." Debbie didn't think he was taking it very seriously.

"Oh come on, Debbie." John winked at her. "I recall a young lady with pink and lime green hair."

Debbie's eyes went wide and her expression clearly signaled her father to not say another word about that, which made him smile. If Debbie thought Grant hadn't heard what her dad had just said, and that maybe her secret rebellious side was safely hidden in the past, that was shattered as soon as they got into the car and headed home.

"You had pink and lime green hair?" Grant snickered.

"Your grandfather is in so much trouble," Debbie replied, which made Grant laugh.

17

John was on his second cup of coffee when he heard Debbie pull into the driveway. Within seconds, she came through the door with Grant in tow. While Debbie stepped over to where John was sitting and kissed his cheek, Grant helped himself to Jan's cup and started making his coffee.

"You let him drink coffee?" Debbie asked, not overly pleased.

"It's okay," John replied with a smirk. "It's really just very sweet cream with a dab of coffee for flavoring."

"He's not allowed coffee at home," Debbie informed her dad and reminded Grant at the same time.

"Good thing that I'm here for the boy then," John replied, which just made Debbie roll her eyes. She kissed Grant's cheek and made for the door. "Try and behave you two."

As soon as Grant heard his mother's car backing out of the drive he said, "This is the eighth day of our project, and she hasn't missed a day of telling us to behave."

"She must somehow feel we need to be reminded."

"Was she like this growing up?" Grant asked.

"Yes and no," John replied. "She was a happy child, and quite creative. A born leader, she always came up with things to do, and all the neighbor girls fell right in line with her plans. Not always for the best. They made forts, went on hunting expeditions, and held a regularly scheduled play of some sort. She wasn't such a creature of routine like she is now, though."

"Regularly scheduled plays?" Grant asked.

"Well, regularly scheduled isn't quite true, but it seemed that every Sunday, she and the neighborhood girls would hold plays that we would have to sit through."

"Boring, huh?"

"Not really, when I think about it, but it always came when I had other things to do," John replied.

"You watched them anyway."

"I did, and I am glad of that now."

"Why is that?" Grant asked.

"Because it showed her how much I cared for her," John smiled at Grant. "It is never the big things that draw people close. Always the day-to-day, mundane things that slowly build a lasting relationship. My stopping what I was doing to watch what she had thrown together told her how important she was to me. It also told her that when she wanted me, I would be there."

"You always look at things in philosophical ways." Grant laughed. "I wish I could do that."

"It comes with age, Son." John laughed. "And keeping your eyes on your priorities."

"What do you mean?"

"In those days, your mother and Wendy were highest on my priority list. They were more important than anything."

"What about Grandma?" Grant asked.

"She was a close second."

140

"She was second?" Grant seemed amazed.

"When you become a parent," John explained. "Nothing is more important than the children. If your grandmother was sitting here instead of me, she would be telling you the same thing. It is the driving force in all of nature. Built into every animal and plant by God, to go forth and multiply. In many creatures, multiplying means their own death, but they do it anyway."

"That's crazy." Grant shook his head.

"Not really, when you think about it." John countered. "The moment we are born, we begin to die, In the human it takes years and decades, but in many species that lifespan is far shorter. If we don't have offspring, we die anyway and all of what we were is forever gone. Take your grandmother as an example. If we had not had a family, she would be just as gone, and I would be sitting here waiting for my death. Because we did have children, I am sitting here visiting with you. Inside of you is a part of who and what your grandmother was. So, in a very real sense, a part of your grandmother lives on and will continue to do so for as long as the family continues."

"Do you see any of Grandma in me?" Grant seemed suddenly serious.

"Actually, I do," John smiled at him.

"Like what?"

"It's little things," John replied. "Like the way you look at things, the things you seem to appreciate, and the way you think of others, and consider their feelings."

Grant had a surprised look on his face, what did his grandfather know? "What do you mean?"

John suddenly realized he might have exposed more of what he knew of the fight than he intended. He did some quick thinking. "Remember the other day out on the boat fishing?"

"Yeah."

"You caught a fish, and you could have just reeled it in but you didn't. You shared that experience with J.J.. Not many people would have done that."

"Sure they would have." Grant shrugged.

"No, they would not have." John corrected. "Not because they wouldn't want to, but simply because they would not have thought to do so. You doing it so automatically showed me that you just naturally think of others and what might bring them pleasure. It is a truly beautiful character trait and one that not many people have. Your grandmother had it, and in you, that trait lives on."

Grant just looked at his papa for a few moments. "Think that would make Grandma proud?"

"I know it would," John smiled. "Mainly, because it makes me proud of you, Son."

They spent the next half hour filling out their to-do list. Then they went out to the garage and inspected the freshly painted chassis. The paint had dried overnight and looked beautiful. John had Grant clean and sand the radiator and shroud while he hand sanded the sheet metal one last time. The radiator and shroud were then painted with a quick drying gloss black paint. While it was drying, they headed off to the local Tractor Supply® store for fluids and other supplies.

While they were loading the engine oil, filter, hydraulic fluid and gear lube, the radiator shop called and told John that his fuel tank was ready for pick up.

"Well, now we have everything we need to complete the project," John said as soon as he closed the phone.

"Another answered prayer." Grant added.

"Only if you were praying for it," John laughed. "I had forgotten about the fuel tank."

"Don't look at me," Grant laughed. "I've lost track of what parts go where. Do you think we're going to be able to put this all back together?"

John laughed. "Putting it back together is the easy part."

"For you maybe," Grant replied. "You sure you know how to put it back together?"

"Of course, I know how," John smiled and looked at Grant. "And how do I know how?"

Grant started to answer with one thing, then laughed and gave another reply. "Because you're a genius."

"There you go."

When they got back to the garage, they unloaded all the parts and supplies. John had them lay everything out on

143

the workbench in the order they would be needed. Then he had Grant help him mount the first rear wheel onto the chassis. While they were doing this, John felt a little light headed, then short of breath, but it seemed to pass. While mounting the last rear wheel onto the chassis, his left arm starting to tingle. He had just tightened the last lug nut when John collapsed on the floor next to the wheel.

"Papa! Papa!" Grant dropped to his knees next to his grandfather and tried to shake him. John's cell phone had slipped out of his shirt pocket when he went down and dropped onto the cement floor. Grant scooped it up and dialed 911. For the next ten minutes, he listened to the emergency operator tell him how to do CPR through the phone's speaker. Every time she asked if he could feel a pulse, he checked and couldn't tell. When the paramedics arrived, they took over. Grant thanked the operator and then called his mother.

As Grant was talking to his mother, Stephanie ran through the door. She stepped up to Grant and waited until his call was finished to find out what happened. She didn't have to wait. After the paramedics shocked John with high voltage, one of them announced that they had a pulse, weak, but a pulse. John was quickly loaded onto a gurney and moved out to the waiting ambulance. Stephanie offered to give Grant a ride to the hospital when she heard him tell his mother to just go to the hospital because he could walk there. If she came and got him first, she wouldn't be at the hospital when Papa got there.

Grant closed the garage and house while Stephanie went back to her house to get her car. The ride to the hospital was a mixture of Grant thanking Stephanie for being there when she was and helping him out, and Stephanie telling him that everything would be all right.

John was still in Emergency when they arrived. Debbie hugged Grant tightly and explained that they were doing tests. At one point she thought that she had heard Papa's voice but couldn't be sure. Grant then introduced Stephanie and stepped back as the two women hugged each other. Half an hour later, a young doctor came out and asked for them to come back. They were led into one of the examining rooms and were shocked by the tubes already running into John's arms and the oxygen mask on his face. John was awake, but not really alert. He looked at Debbie, Grant, and Stephanie, but they couldn't tell if their presence registered in his mind.

"He has had a serious heart attack." The doctor explained. "We have found a clogged artery that caused it, but there could be more problems."

"What are you going to do?" Grant asked.

"We need to do surgery as soon as possible." The doctor answered.

"Yes, please do it now." Debbie was almost in tears. "Are you going to do a by-pass?"

"I'm not sure just yet." The doctor replied. "We have a new procedure where we can go into the artery and clear away the blockage. Then we insert a stint that will keep the artery open. We are having an operating room prepared now."

When they came down to the ER to get John and take him upstairs, Debbie was able to hold her dad's hand and kiss his check. John wasn't able to speak, but he did manage to _wink_ at her. When they wheeled him into the elevator, the doctor told them that the procedure would take a couple of hours and that the three of them should go down to the cafeteria and get something to eat and drink."

"Where will you take him after the procedure?" Stephanie asked.

"He will be taken to recovery, and there's a waiting room just outside." The doctor said.

Stephanie wrapped her arms around both Debbie and Grant and turned them away from the elevator. "Let's let the doctor do his magic while we follow his advice. Stephanie treated them to lunch and when they had found a table and sat down, Grant asked his mom if she had called Wendy?

Debbie's face paled and she almost jumped to her feet and made for a quiet corner of the cafeteria, dialing her phone as she went. For ten minutes Debbie paced back and forth talking with her sister. The entire time tears were running down her cheeks.

Stephanie noticed Grant as he kept checking on his mother. "Your grandfather will be okay, I am sure of it." She told him. He just looked at her and nodded. "He is quite a man, your grandfather."

"Yes he is," Grant agreed.

"It'll take him some time to recover, but you being there when it happened made all the difference. You saved his life."

Grant just looked up at her; he knew his grandfather would be dead now if all he had to rely on was his own

146

knowledge and skill. "I didn't know what I was doing." Grant replied. "The 911 operator had to talk me through it. When Papa is better, I am going to learn CPR."

"You did CPR until the paramedics got there?"

"Yes, with the operator's help."

"Then you really did save your grandfather's life!" Stephanie said.

"She's right, Grant," Debbie said as she took her place at the table again. "I am very proud of what you did."

"You two are making too much of it." Grant said. "Is Wendy coming home?"

"She wants to but is not sure she can right away. I promised to call her tonight and then again in the morning after I've seen Dad."

18

Three hours after John was wheeled into surgery, the doctor finally came into the waiting room looking for Debbie. The doctor was cautiously optimistic. John had made it through the procedure just fine. He had three clogged arteries. One of which was 90% blocked, but luckily the other two were much less. All three had been cleared and stints installed. The doctor explained that John was in recovery and then would be brought into ICU, and Debbie could see him for a few minutes after they got him settled in.

Grant asked if he would be able to see his grandfather. The doctor looked at him and took in the fact that Grant was dressed in his old work clothes. Trying to be polite, the doctor said that they were going to limit the visitors to one for now. He also noted that he might have a chance in the morning, but he would have to be clean to get in. Infections were a real threat at the moment. Grant nodded that he understood.

When the doctor left the room, Stephanie stepped up to Debbie and gave her a tight hug and told her to tell her dad that he was being prayed for. Debbie nodded and smiled through a tear streaked face, and thanked Stephanie for being there when they needed her. As Stephanie turned to leave, Grant stopped her and asked if he could catch a ride back to Papa's. Before she answered that, she glanced over at his mother for her decision.

Debbie looked at her son with a surprised expression. "Grant, you need to stay here with me."

Grant stepped closer to his mother. "I understand how you feel Mom, I really do. You heard the doctor, they are not going to let me see Papa tonight and there is something very important that I must do at Papa's tonight. I have to do this, for him and for me."

"No Grant," Debbie was shaking her head. "I don't want you over there by yourself working on that old tractor."

"I understand your concern, Mom. I really do, but all the heavy lifting and dangerous stuff is already done. Also, if I don't do what I need to do tonight, I can't surprise Papa when he gets to go home. Mom, I'm asking you to trust me. For once in our lives, please just trust me. You can pick me up on your way home."

Debbie looked deep into her son's eyes. She wanted to trust him, but he had let her down so many times before. She closed her eyes and nodded. Grant bent down and kissed her cheek. "Don't let me down."

"I won't Mom, I promise." Grant replied. "Oh, and don't mention this to Papa."

On the way back to John's, Stephanie asked Grant what was so important that he had to accomplish it that night? He explained that Papa and he were restoring the old tractor that his father had owned.

"How is that coming?"

"We had planned on finishing it tomorrow." Grant replied. "And that is a plan I am going to keep."

"Do you need any help?" Stephanie asked.

Grant looked at her with a surprised look in his eye and she caught it.

"I'm not really mechanically inclined," Stephanie laughed. "I can help lift things or hold things if you need a hand."

"Actually, I don't." Grant replied. "Not tonight anyway. I have to get the sheet metal parts painted so they can dry overnight and be ready to assemble tomorrow."

"Well, be careful," Stephanie said. "I am going to give you my phone number when I drop you off, just in case."

The first thing Grant did when he got into the garage was check over Papa's to-do list. He carefully checked off the things they had gotten done. He then moved on to the next item on the list and installed the front wheels and tires. The radiator was next in line. Luckily he had helped take it off, and he remembered how it went back on. He then found the fan belt, radiator hoses and clamps that Papa had purchased. The next item on the list was to add coolant, but how much? He took the time to search for the manual John had bought and then spent several more minutes finding the capacities page. He added a gallon of coolant and then a gallon of water before adding another gallon of coolant.

Finally, he reached the point on the list for the painting of the sheet metal. He mixed the strange gray colored paint just as Papa had taught him. After donning his respirator, he sprayed the first light coat. He started with the inside and slowly moved around the rack, making sure to get a light, even coat under all of the pieces. Painting the outside was much easier, but also, the most stressful because it would show to the world when done.

To spend the time while he was waiting for that first coat to flash, he took Papa's digital camera and started going through the pictures stored on the camera's chip. He clicked all the way back to when they started tearing the tractor apart. His Papa had insisted that they capture each step. It was something that he really appreciated right now. He also read through parts of the service manual. His biggest concern at the moment was wiring the tractor with the 12-volt system his grandfather had bought.

After the second coat, he went back to clicking through the pictures. Numerous things came to mind as he contemplated what lay ahead of him to put this tractor back together by himself. He had to complete it before Papa came home from the hospital. Tomorrow was the goal date to finish.

As Grant sat there in the gathering darkness, he realized how far over his head he was. That morning when his papa had collapsed, and he was trying to keep him alive until the paramedics got there, Grant had earnestly prayed for the first time in his life. He now wondered if God had answered that prayer, or if the 911 operator was responsible for Papa being still among the living. Grant slowly looked up into the darkening night sky.

"God, I don't know how to go about this. Honestly, I am not sure what I believe. I know my papa believes in you, and he is a really good man. I want to believe you heard me this morning and spared Papa's life. I also know that if you are real, I am not worthy of your time, but my papa is. God, I can't do this without your help. Please help me do this right, for Papa. Thank you, God."

151

The final coat was the one he had been the most worried about. He carefully sprayed it on as Papa had shown him on the chassis when they had painted that. He kept the gun moving to avoid getting a run or puddling it. He was just cleaning out the gun when his mother came through the door. She told him that she was outside, and quickly retreated out the door into the fresh night air. Grant followed her out the door a couple of minutes later.

"How did it go?" Debbie asked her son.

"Finished Papa's to-do list for today." Grant replied proudly. "Everything Papa thought we would have to accomplish today in order to finish the project tomorrow."

"The tractor was going to be finished tomorrow?" Debbie was surprised.

"It's going to be finished, Mom." Grant corrected her.

"Grant, we need to spend time at the hospital with Grandpa."

"I was hoping we could go in the morning," Grant replied. "And then you could bring me here."

"This is very important to you isn't it?"

"Mom, this is the most important thing I've ever done for anyone." Grant replied. "I want to do this for Papa, but I also need to do this for me."

"Are you done for tonight?" Debbie asked.

"I am," Grant nodded. "Ready to go home. I do have a request."

"And what is that?"

"Can I borrow your computer tonight?"

"Something you're not sure of?" Debbie raised an eyebrow.

Grant smiled at her. "Several things actually. Mainly, the wiring."

"You're going to wire that tractor?"

Grant laughed. "I am. Before I do, however, I have to figure out how."

"Let's get home," Debbie turned toward her car. "Jason knows a few people in the old car hobby, maybe he can help by getting you in touch with some of them.

19

When Debbie and Grant came through the door at home, Jason had their supper all ready for them and had already fed J.J.. He looked up from his task of cleaning the active little guy up. "How is your father?"

Debbie went into detail about what had happened and what procedure the doctors used to clear the blockage. While she was explaining all of this, she dished a plate of goulash up for Grant, and then one for Jason, then finally one for herself. She proudly told Jason how Grant had saved his grandfather's life.

"That's awesome Grant! I'm really impressed." Jason meant it.

"There's one other thing," Debbie added, once all three of them had sat down to eat.

"What's that?" Jason asked as he took his first bite.

"Grant needs your help."

"Oh, in what way?" Jason seemed confused.

"He is planning on finishing that old tractor that he and Dad have been working on," Debbie explained. "And he needs some expert advice about wiring."

"I don't know the first thing about wiring," Jason admitted.

"No, but you know people that do." Debbie countered. "Who do you know close by that would help him understand what he has to do tomorrow?"

"Tomorrow?" Jason was surprised and looked at Grant. "Aren't you going to see your grandfather at the hospital?"

"I plan on seeing him in the morning." Grant replied. "I can't stay there all day, and I am sure that the hospital wouldn't want me there that long either. I really want to finish this project for Papa."

"I don't know of anyone I could ask to help you tomorrow," Jason replied. "Everyone I do know has to work tomorrow, maybe Saturday."

"I don't want them to help me do the work." Grant explained. "I just need someone that could go over it tonight. Explain to me what I need to understand and do."

Jason thought a moment before getting up from the table, pulling his phone out and scrolling through some numbers before dialing one of them. He stepped out of the kitchen just as the person he had dialed answered the call. Two minutes later, he came into the kitchen with his phone back in his pocket and a smile on his face.

"Billy Smith said for you to come right over," Jason said to Grant. "He lives just four houses down on the other side of the street."

"Is he the guy in the white house with black shutters, and always has real old cars in the driveway?"

"That's him." Jason nodded. "He said that he would be glad to help you out. He is in the garage behind the house right now."

Grant was out of his chair and scooping up the bag of things he had brought home from Papa's. "Thanks, I really appreciate your help."

"Just don't stay over there too late," Debbie said. "I'll leave the goulash out until you get back, that way if you're still hungry, you can microwave another plate."

"I'm fine Mom, thanks." Grant replied as he bolted out the door. In minutes, he was walking up the driveway. Light was escaping under the roll-up garage door, and from the square window in the passage door to the left of the big door. Grant opened the passage door far enough to stick his head in. He saw a man, closer to Papa's age than Jason's, bent over a highly chromed V8 engine mounted in the front end of a really cool looking hot rod.

"You Billy?" Grant asked.

The man turned around. He was tall and thin and dressed in a dark blue auto service uniform. "I am. Are you Grant?"

"Yes, sir." Grant replied as he stepped through the door. "I really appreciate your help."

"We all had to start somewhere, and lean on someone else to teach us what we didn't know," Billy smiled and reached out and shook Grant's hand. "Come with me." Billy led Grant over to the long maple work bench that looked like it had been made from the remains of some old bowling alley. He pulled two barstools out and motioned for Grant to have a seat. "Jason said you were working on an old tractor, something about your grandfather having a heart attack and you wanting to complete the job for him."

156

"Yes, that's about the size of it." Grant answered. "The tractor has a lot of meaning to my grandfather. His father bought it new in 1953."

"Is it a Jubilee?" Billy interrupted.

"Yes," Grant nodded, surprised that an old car guy would know about an old tractor.

"Great tractor," Billy smiled. "Sorry to interrupt, please continue."

"Anyway," Grant went on. "It was also the first tractor my grandfather ever drove. In fact, he was driving it the day he got his first date with my grandmother. She just died a month ago."

"I'm sorry to hear that." Billy frowned.

"So, I got expelled from school for two weeks, and my mother sends me to Papa's. We decided to spend our time together restoring the Jubilee."

"Two quick questions," Billy stopped him a moment. "First, what were you expelled for?"

"Fighting."

"Was it worth it?"

"I should have found a better way to handle the situation, I know that now," Grant admitted. "To tell the truth, however, I wouldn't have missed these past two weeks for anything. I really got to know and love my papa. I can't explain it, but for the first time in my life I feel I really know him, and I think he knows me just as well."

"That's cool man, way cool."

"What was the second question?" Grant asked.

"Was a girl involved?"

"Not directly." Grant answered instantly, almost like he had rehearsed this answer.

Billy looked at the boy for several seconds, "Oookay." When Grant offered nothing more, Billy got down to business. "What can I do to help you out?"

"We are at the assembly stage of the restoration. The chassis is painted, the sheet metal is all painted, and hopefully that dries well tonight."

"Just painted it today?" Billy asked. "Ever paint before?"

"Not without my papa standing over my shoulder." Grant smiled. "But, I had no choice. If I didn't paint it tonight, it wouldn't be dry tomorrow."

"How did it look when you left?"

"Really good." Grant replied.

"Then I am sure it will be just fine," Billy assured him. "Now what is your biggest concern?"

"Papa bought a 12-volt conversion for the tractor. It includes brackets, an alternator that Papa called one wire, and an internally resisted coil, whatever that means." Grant shrugged. "What it didn't include was new wiring or instructions on how to do it."

"What do you understand about current or wiring?" Billy asked.

"Nothing." Grant was honest. "I do have pictures of the old electrical system as we took it out."

"Oh, can I see them?"

Grant reached into the bag and pulled Papa's camera out and started looking back through the pictures until he came to the wiring. He then handed the camera over to Billy.

Billy quickly flipped through the pictures until he found what he was looking for. "See this little junction here?" He pointed to the center of the picture where there were two small bolts situated close to each other and with each having wires attached to them.

"Yeah, I see it." Grant remembered taking that picture and knew exactly what Billy was referring to.

"That, my young friend, is going to make your life easy." Billy laughed as he reached up and grabbed his notebook and a #2 pencil. In less than a minute, he had drawn out the entire electrical system on a Ford Jubilee tractor. Then, as an extra added feature, he wrote one of only three different numbers on each wire in the diagram, either a 10, 12, or 14 to identify the gauge of wire to be used. For the next ten minutes, Billy went over the diagram until Grant had it down pat.

"Okay, beyond the electrical, any other issues I could help with?"

"On the list Papa made out a couple of days ago, it says 'rebuild carburetor'. Grant replied.

"That's probably an old Marvel updraft." Billy smiled as he flipped through the images on the camera

159

looking for one of the carburetor. "Okay, here it is." He said as he looked the unit over. "If you have the rebuild kit already, I am sure your grandfather ordered it by the model number. These are very easy to rebuild. Just lay them out as you take it apart. Then use brake-clean to clean it out and carefully put it back together in the reverse order you took it apart. Just be sure to shoot a strong shot through each and every orifice. If it doesn't shoot out as much as you're shooting in, you have a blockage. Try high-pressure air. You do have a compressor, right?"

"Yes."

"Most carb kits come with instructions, so follow those. Just remember, the main thing is that every jet needs to be open. Change out the needle and seat. That's the brass barrel with a slot running through it, and the smaller brass bob, the needle in the middle of it. Change them out, just be sure to find a wide enough tool to engage the slots on both sides of the bowl. Check the float in a bucket of water to be sure it doesn't leak. You'll see bubbles if it does. And finally, change the main gasket and the manifold gasket. The manifold gasket is the one between the carburetor and the base throat of the manifold, right here." Billy showed Grant the spot on the photograph by pointing it out.

He finally went into how to adjust the carburetor for the initial start-up. Then Grant asked about polarizing the electrical system, he had just remembered reading about that.

Billy laughed. "That's the trouble with installing a modern charging system using 60-year-old manuals. The modern alternator system you are installing doesn't require polarizing. What's that popular term used these days for electronics, plug and play?"

160

"Yeah, plug and play."

"That's all you have to do with this system your grandfather bought. I have the same charging system on this 32 Highboy." Billy said with a wave of his hand toward the hotrod he had been working on.

"Really?" Grant was surprised that this cool car would have anything in common with their tractor.

"Come here," Billy motioned for Grant to follow him as he got off his stool and walked over to the car. He bent down on the right side of the car and pointed out the alternator. "Take a picture of this because you will wire yours just like this."

Grant took the picture and then noticed something. "That wiring looks like it is factory made."

Billy smiled and patted Grant on the back. "Yours will too because I am going to show you how."

Billy explained how to attach terminal ends and shrink wrap, and even had Grant make a couple so they were both sure he would know what he was doing. Finally, Billy laid his hands on Grants shoulders. "What I am about to share with you now is the best-kept secret of automotive electrical systems."

"Okay." Grant felt nervous about what was to come.

"If you have an electrical fault, check your ground. If you still have an electrical fault, check your ground. And then if you still have an electrical problem, check your ground."

"So the ground is important." Grant joked.

161

Billy roared with laughter. "Ground is 99.9% of all electrical problems. Which reminds me, when installing the rear fenders, grind a small area on the bottom of the fender and a matching small area on the top of the axle. The point where the two make contact. Then be sure the light fixtures have a good ground where they mate to the fenders. It's all about ground. No ground, no lights."

"Ground, ground, ground," Grant confirmed.

"You'll do great tomorrow, Son." Billy slapped him on the back.

When Grant finally headed for home, he had been at Billy's for just under two hours. Billy had taught him a lot in such a short time and loaned him some special tools and supplies to make the job look great. The best part of all was that Billy promised to stop by John's house after work and check on how it was going. That alone filled Grant with confidence.

Another hour and a half was spent on the computer when he got home. He printed off a dozen pages and had several more pages of notes that he had jotted down. Debbie and Jason exchanged glances while watching Grant search the internet for information. Debbie had never seen Grant go after something with this much enthusiasm and dedication. Her father's words from a week ago suddenly hit home. "I can't promise Grant will be a new boy when he goes back to school. Nor can I promise he'll be a new boy in a week or a month, but in time, Grant's own time. These two weeks will be remembered as time well spent." She realized that she could already see a change in her son. As she watched Grant working, she also realized that she could see her father in him. Her father was always a man with a purpose. He had always told her about the 5 p's. She

162

had to smile because she didn't remember what they all were, but she did remember planning and performance were two of them.

Grant suddenly seemed to run out of steam. He collected his notes and turned the computer off.

"Find everything you need?" Debbie asked.

"Got my plan right here." Grant smiled. "Even put together my 'to-do' list."

"The 5 p's," Debbie said, wondering if her father had passed that little trait along to her son.

"Prior-Planning-Prevents-Poor-Performance." Grant smiled as he stood up.

Debbie had to laugh. She really could see her father in Grant. "Well, Son. You better get to bed. You have a full day ahead of you tomorrow."

No argument from Grant, as had been his usual response. Instead, he stepped up to his mother and kissed her cheek. "Goodnight Mom, and thank you for understanding. Goodnight Jason." With that, Grant turned and moved down the hall to his bedroom, and in less than two minutes the light was out.

"You know," Jason said after Grant was in bed. "I told the boss that I was going to be in late tomorrow because I needed to stop by the hospital. Why don't I take Grant to your dad's place after, that way you can stay at the hospital with your dad?"

"You don't mind?"

"No, I really don't, and I would like to see this tractor anyway."

20

The following morning, Grant rode with his mother to the hospital as Jason took little J.J. to the sitter's. Expectations were high as they rode the elevator up to ICU. When Debbie had left the hospital the night before, her father was sitting up and talking with her and in good spirits. Things couldn't have been more different when they stepped off the elevator at ICU. The nurses were rushing around getting John ready for by-pass surgery. During the night, the stint in the artery that had been severely blocked had ruptured and started leaking. The doctor explained to Debbie that the leak wasn't much, but enough to warrant going in and replacing the bad section of artery. They would be taking what they needed from his leg.

After putting a paper gown and mask on, both Grant and Debbie were allowed a few seconds at John's side. He was drowsy but awake. He held Debbie's hand and tried to smile at her. After she kissed his forehead, John looked at Grant and motioned for him to step closer. Grant stepped up to his papa's side and took the hand being offered. John's face was covered with a clear plastic breathing mask. Despite that, the two looked deeply into each other's eyes, and when John squeezed Grant's hand firmly, Grant squeezed back. Not a word was spoken, none was needed. They both felt the bond and the love they now shared.

As they were firmly holding hands, the nurses began to move the gurney toward the elevator. While doing so, they informed Grant that it was time to go. Grant released his Papa's hand and stood back as the nurses pushed Papa away from him. Grant could see his papa trying to keep his eyes on him. Then he saw Papa raise his right hand slightly off the gurney and give Grant the thumbs up sign, which Grant returned with a smile. The two kept their eyes locked on one another until the doors of the elevator closed and blocked their sight. Grant slowly turned around and almost bumped into his mother. She had been right behind him and had witnessed the entire thing. Grant put his arm around her shoulder and led her out of the ICU to the waiting room.

Jason wasn't there yet, so Grant helped his mother out of her paper gown and sat with her quietly holding her hand. "I was very touched by the sight of you and your grandfather just now," Debbie said while she squeezed his hand.

"I think he knows what I am doing." Grant replied.

"Why, did he say something?"

"He didn't have to. I saw it in his eyes." Grant said. "I could also feel it in his grip."

"Is that what the thumbs-up was about?"

"Yeah." Grant smiled at her.

"So you still want to go back to the garage this morning?" Debbie asked, making Grant quickly take stock of the situation.

"A part of me feels I should be here with you," Grant admitted. "I realize that, but I also realize that there is nothing I can do here. Everything is in the doctor's hands. I felt Papa's blessing and feel like I need to go to work. I have Papa's phone so you can reach me at any time." Debbie just looked at him, and slowly nodded her head.

Jason arrived and listened while his wife tearfully explained what had transpired with her father. He told her that he was going to call into work and take the day off to be with her. In the meantime, he would run Grant over to John's. Debbie hugged Jason and then Grant, telling him to be careful. He promised that he would be.

When they arrived at the garage, Jason followed Grant in and was blown away by the transformation. He had not seen the old tractor since the garage sale and couldn't believe what a difference two weeks had made. While Jason was looking the bright red chassis over, Grant had walked over to the sheet metal rack and was carefully examining the paint job he had done the night before. The paint was dry and yet had a wet-look gloss to it, which made Grant really smile, Papa would approve.

"Is this what you painted last night?" Jason asked as he stepped over to the paint jig.

"Yeah." Grant answered.

"Wow! This looks great! I didn't know you could paint like this." Jason was truly impressed.

"I painted the chassis over there." Grant nodded toward the red chassis. "That was with Papa standing over my shoulder talking me through it. This was different, this was on my own, but I could hear him in my head the whole time. So, in a way, he was right beside me helping."

"Well, I know he is going to be very proud of you." Jason patted Grant on the back. "You've done a really nice job of it. Do you need any help putting these parts together and on the tractor?"

"No, not right now." Grant replied. "I have a ton of things to do before I can even get to that, but thanks for asking."

"Okay, I will let you get to it," Jason said. "You have your grandfather's phone, so call if you need me."

"I will," Grant promised. "And you call me when you know something about Papa."

"We will, I promise."

After Jason left, Grant laid his notes out on the work bench. On top of the notes was his very first to-do list that he had made out himself. He was nervous and excited about what lie before him. He suddenly realized that something was missing, coffee. He decided to go get the coffee maker and bring it out to the garage. He easily found the coffee jar and the filters but had no idea how much coffee to put into the filter to brew a pot of coffee. The best he could come up with was remembering that when his mother made coffee, it appeared to him that the filter was about half full of ground coffee. With nothing else to go on, that is what he did. He carried the coffee maker out to the garage, filled it with water and went back into the house to get himself a cup and the cream and sugar.

The cups that he and Papa had used the morning before had not been washed and were sitting in the kitchen sink. Grant reached for his, then changed his mind and picked up Papa's. That would be the cup he would use today. He grabbed the cream out of the refrigerator and the bowl of sugar from the counter and headed for the garage. The brewing coffee smelled wonderful but yielded the strongest tasting coffee he had ever had.

The first item on the list was to install the gauges into the dash panel. Grant carefully removed the dash panel from his painting jig. Then he opened the four little boxes containing the gauges and secured them into place with the enclosed brackets. Then the grommets for the steering column and the throttle rod were installed, followed by the throttle rod itself and finally the lower dress panel. Papa had purchased all new zinc coated screws to fasten everything together, making assembly pretty straight-forward and easy. He carefully slid the dash panel over the steering column and screwed it into place. Item number one on the list was completed. Grant took a few moments to stand back and admire the job. The dash and gauges looked great.

Next, on the list was connecting the temperature and oil pressure gauges. A website he had visited the night before recommended doing these before the wiring because they were less flexible, while wiring could be molded around to fit several different ways. The oil pressure line was the first of the two to be installed. To be installed correctly, both little threaded couplers at the ends of the line had to be lined up perfectly with the fittings they screwed into. He remembered his papa cautioning him to be careful not to cross-thread any brass fittings because the brass threads were weak and could easily be stripped, ruining the fittings. To be certain not to cross thread them, he gently tried to thread them by hand. It took numerous tries and over half an hour to get the threads lined up so that they would thread in without stripping. He was hoping and praying that the temperature sending unit would go smoother.

He threaded the flexible temperature line around the bracket that held the fuel tank to the right side of the engine. The temperature line was much longer than was needed, and he wondered how he would hide that extra line. He decided to deal with that later when the fuel tank was installed. It took him three trips to the tool box to find the right wrench for removing the old sending unit, which had been left in the engine to prevent paint from getting inside when they painted the chassis. It wasn't until he started removing the old sending unit, that he realized that removing it would open the cooling system up, and all the new coolant he had installed yesterday would leak out. He thought about pulling the old one out and trying to install the new one quick enough to prevent a lot of coolant loss. While that would have been much quicker, it would have created a mess, and probably the loss of more coolant than he could afford to lose. Grant decided to do it right and drain the coolant down first so the job could be done without making a mess and losing coolant. The extra time that it took made him wonder if he had a prayer of completing the to-do list by the end of the day.

Finally, the sending unit and the coolant were back in, and the slight mess he had made doing the job was cleaned up so he wouldn't track it all over the garage. Now came the part that had caused him the most concern, wiring the tractor. Twenty-four hours ago he was pretty sure it was out of his abilities. Now, thanks to Billy, he was pretty sure he could do it. Billy had recommended doing the hardest to get to things first. Since the amp gauge was the hardest to see anyway, Grant decided that he would wire that first. Before even starting, he decided that two things had to be done. He filled his coffee cup with coffee, and taped Billy's diagram to the side of the engine. He took a swallow of coffee while studying the diagram that showed three 10 gauge wires being attached to the amp gauge. One from the positive terminal that ran to the alternator. Two 10 gauge wires that ran from the negative side of the gauge. One of those went to one side of the junction terminal, and the other to the battery side of the starter solenoid.

Well, the diagram didn't make it seem all that terribly difficult, so Grant took the three ten foot rolls of red insulated 10 gauge wire that John had gotten and rolled them out. He then carefully cut three small pieces of shrink wrap and slid that over the ends of the wire. Then he stripped the wires back about half an inch. Then he found three yellow tipped eyelet terminal ends that fit snuggly to the posts on the amp gauge. Following what Billy had taught him, he took the ends over to the bench grinder and ground enough off the yellow plastic until it slipped off the end. The ends were then slipped over the wire and crimped tightly. Grant tugged on the ends to be certain of a tight fit. Then the shrink was slid over the crimped part of the end, and using a mini torch Billy had loaned him, he heated the wrap until it shrank tightly around the wire and the end giving a professional look.

Once he had them securely attached to the back of the gauge, he ran them out to where they were to go and cut the wires to length and repeated the process with terminal ends and shrink wrap. Before installing the end to the alternator wire, however, he cut a piece of wiring loom that Billy had given him. Billy had called it old-school because it was of a tar impregnated woven material. When that was completed, Grant had to stand back and admire it. It really did look like a professional had done it. Next, he installed the ignition switch and wired that in according to the diagram. Then came the light switch and the wires leading to where the headlights and tail light would be. Finally, he ran the wire to the coil, and then another short one from the coil to the distributor.

Suddenly, he realized that just two items down the to-do list was to install the fuel tank, and it hadn't even been painted yet. He quickly set the fuel tank up on a couple of sawhorses and wiped the outside down with thinner as he had seen John do. Then he looked through his papa's paints and found a quick drying hammered silver. Thinking the tank would look nice in that color, and it didn't seem too far away from what it was originally. Grant painted the tank, then hung it up from the garage door frame so he could get the bottom side.

He took a quick look around at the parts waiting to be installed and read through the to-do list again. He didn't want to come across anything like the fuel tank again. If he hadn't caught it when he did, he would have been standing around waiting for paint to dry. The next two items on the list were to install the tachometer drive cable and the alternator and brackets. The tach cable went on in seconds, but he had a bit of a problem getting the alternator brackets on the right way so the alternator pulley and the fan belt lined up perfectly. After a ten-minute struggle, the alternator was in place and he quickly connected the wiring end he had made for it.

He crossed those two items off the list and decided to skip over installing the fuel tank for a moment. Instead, he would install the manifold and the exhaust system. He found the gaskets and the brass washers and nuts that held the manifold in place. Luckily, Papa had already cleaned and painted the manifold in a flat black he called Header black. He had explained at the time that the paint was special temperature resistant paint. Grant laid the manual out on the floor, weighed down with a heavy wrench, so he could refer to it as he worked.

After he installed the manifold and exhaust system, Grant went over to the fuel tank and lightly tested the finish. It was still a little bit tacky so he moved on to the next item on the list. Rebuilding the carburetor. Billy had given some good pointers on this, and the manual was fairly detailed with good pictures. In less than twenty minutes, Grant had rebuilt his first carburetor. This he painted it an antique cast finish and set it aside to dry.

The battery box and the battery cables were next in line so he quickly installed them and then installed the still a bit tacky fuel tank. With each item that was installed and each item crossed off the to-do list, Grant was getting more and more excited. He was really beginning to see the light at the end of the tunnel. He could do this! Wouldn't Papa be impressed to walk in and see the finished tractor?

Grant carefully installed the fuel line and carburetor with all its linkage. He tried the choke and the throttle, and both seemed to work just fine. He stepped back a moment and looked his handiwork over. He knew he was just moments away from starting this thing up, and then he spotted the jugs of oil and lube sitting where they had sat them down when they carried them into the garage. Grant's heart skipped a beat. He suddenly realized that if he had tried to start the tractor without the oil and other fluids installed, he would have ruined Papa's tractor in a second. He scolded himself for being careless. He quickly read through the manual about where to install what fluids and how much. When he finished installing the fluids and the engine oil filter, he realized that he didn't have any gas for the engine. He looked through the garage and found Papa's

173

gas can for the lawnmower. It was empty. He knew there was a service station just five or six blocks from the garage, and he had about ten dollars in his pocket, hopefully, that would be enough.

On the way back from the service station carrying two and a half gallons of gas, Grant was glad that he didn't have $20.00 on him. This much gas was heavy enough after four blocks. After carrying the gas six blocks, he finally got back to the garage and started to pour the gas into the fuel tank, when it splattered all over the new paint job and instantly lifted the new paint. Grant frowned and thought that there was nothing to be done about it now, so he kept pouring the fuel in. While he was holding the fuel can, he glanced down at the engine and noticed something wasn't S P quite right. Then he realized that there were no spark plug wires and the old painted plugs were still in the engine.

Once the fuel can was empty, Grant carefully touched up the paint on the tank and went in search of the new spark plugs and wires he knew they had. He found them in a box with other parts he realized that he would need to install as well. The problem was, he didn't know where they went until he searched through the manual. They had good pictures and an equally good explanation of how to install the points, condenser, rotor, and plug wires. He found a small metal tab packaged with the points that had .020" stamped on the side of it, and sure enough, the directions explained what it was for. The last step was to install the battery itself and tighten the cables.

He was finally ready for the big moment. It was time to open up the fuel valve and test fire the tractor's engine. The valve opened smoothly, the ignition key turned smoothly, the stick shift wobbled safely from side to side to ensure it was in neutral. Then Grant held his breath and reached down and slowly depressed the starter button. He was expecting the engine to spin over and roar to life, instead nothing! Not a sound, nothing. Grant couldn't believe it, he had been so careful, following his to-do list to the letter. He had done everything the manual had said. He glanced over at Billy's diagram, now laying on the work bench. He followed every wire, he had correctly done them all. Or had he? He spotted one that he had missed. The 12 gauge wire that ran from the starter button to the starter solenoid.

Grant smiled and looked up at the ceiling. "Is that you teasing me Lord? Not such a hot-shot after all, am I?" It took only a couple of minutes to make up the wire and run it. The next time Grant hit the starter button, the starter engaged and spun the engine easily. In a matter of only a few revolutions, the engine caught and roared to life. Grant quickly checked the tach, engine RPM below 1,000, good, just like Billy had told him to do. The oil pressure was dead on 40, just what he expected to find. The amp gauge showed a charge of 10 amps. He didn't know if that was good, but at least, it was charging. The temperature gauge hadn't budged, but he hadn't really expected it to. He was familiar enough with the temperature gauges in cars to know that it takes a few minutes for the engine to warm up.

While looking at the gauges and listening to the engine run so smoothly, Grant didn't notice the blue smoke from the exhaust pipe at first. When he finally did notice it, the interior of the garage was in a fog. He quickly stepped over to the big overhead door and pushed the button to raise it. In seconds, the smoke was billowing out the door while inside the garage the smoke was clearing out.

Grant left the engine run until the temperature gauge started climbing. He wanted to be sure it would reach a point and then stop. While his eyes were glued to the gauge he didn't see Stephanie running up the drive with a fire extinguisher in hand.

21

Grants eyes were glued to the gauges. Twice he had glanced back at the tip of the tailpipe watching for the blue smoke to burn itself out. When he was helping Papa rebuild the engine, all the moving parts were coated in a slimy dark pink slime that Papa had called assembly lube. At the time, Papa had explained that the lube was important because when they did start the engine, it would take a few seconds for the oil pump to build a good running pressure and be able to keep everything lubricated. The slimy assembly lube would do that job until regular engine oil took over the task. "It'll blow smoke until the assembly lube is burned off," Papa had told him. The longer the engine ran, the lighter the smoke from the pipe became. After a short time, the exhaust cleared up entirely.

Grant hadn't seen Stephanie running up the driveway with the fire extinguisher, nor had he seen her enter the garage and sit the extinguisher down. He had just checked the tailpipe and was turning to inspect the gauges when he caught movement in his peripheral vision. Before he could fully turn to see who it was, Stephanie wrapped her arms around him, and tightly hugged him. She was beyond excited to see that he had the tractor running and nearly jumping up and down with him locked in her arms. Adults could be very strange sometimes, Grant thought.

When Stephanie finally released her arm lock on Grant, he automatically stepped back until he felt the side of the tractor against his back. He slowly reached out with his right hand, feeling for, and then finding the ignition switch and switching the engine off. Stephanie was all smiles until the engine died.

"Is everything okay?" She asked.

"Yeah," Grant smiled. "I don't have much gas in it, and I just needed to run it long enough to test the systems and burn off the assembly lube."

"Is that what caused all the smoke?"

"Yeah."

"I was in my back yard when I heard something, I didn't think it would be this tractor running," Stephanie explained. "Then I saw a billow of smoke coming from this garage and was afraid something bad had happened."

"I'm sorry," Grant shyly smiled. "I didn't mean to cause concern."

"Oh, don't you worry about that." Stephanie was all smiles again. "I am just so excited for you! Your grandfather is going to be so proud of you. I just can't believe it! And it looks so beautiful. I know it's missing a lot of parts yet, but what is here looks beautiful."

"Here's the rest of it." Grant led her over to the paint jig. "This is what I had to do last night."

"You painted these parts last night? By yourself?"

"Yeah."

"Oh, honey!" Stephanie wrapped her arms around him again and squeezed the stuffing out of him. "I'm so proud of you, I know your grandfather is going to be."

"It is coming along," Grant admitted. "There is a lot to do yet before it is finished, though." He was proud of himself for not saying what he really meant, that he wanted to get back to work.

③ Stephanie turned and looked at him a moment, then reached up and pinched his cheek. "I'll let you get back to it then. Just call me if you need anything, okay?"

"Okay." Grant replied while wondering why so many women pinched his cheeks. It might have been cute when he was little, but now they had to reach up to do it. His mother always told him that women did it because they thought he was cute. "Cute." He sighed while shaking his head. The thought of his mother made him wonder how Papa was doing, so he stepped outside the garage and dialed his mother's cell phone. She answered on the third ring.

"Everything okay Grant?"

"Yeah, going really well. How is Papa?"

"He is in recovery right now," Debbie answered. "The surgery took longer than expected, but the doctor said that everything went well."

"Good, I was beginning to get worried." Grant said. "Remember not to say anything about what I am doing."

"I thought you said he knows." Debbie seemed confused.

"I think he knows," Grant corrected. "Not positive. If he doesn't know, I would like to keep it that way."

"Okay." Debbie agreed. "You sure you're okay?"

"Doing great Mom. I just had it running."

"You did! Holy Cow! I am so proud of you Grant. And I am sure Papa will be even more so."

"Thanks, Mom."

179

"Just be careful."

"Yes Mom, I will be. " Grant had to smile. If only he had a nickel for every time his mother had told him to be careful or be good.

The next item on the to-do list was to mount the headlight buckets to the front fenders. Following Billy's instructions, Grant made sure that where the headlight contacted against the fender, namely where the bolt went through the fender, a small space was scratched down to bare metal on both the fender and the thick support washer. Once both buckets were securely installed, Grant opened the new headlight boxes and examined the bulbs. At the back of the bulbs were two small brass screws. Grant had learned enough over the last 24 hours to know that he needed to run his power line to one, and connect the other to a good ground. Luckily, when they took the original bulbs out of the buckets, the ground wires in both were in good condition and still securely connected to the inside of the buckets. All Grant had to do was make a new positive wire and feed it through the hole in the center on the mounting bolt. As a final added touch, also one Billy suggested. Grant installed plug connectors to the end of the positive headlight leads. That would allow the headlights to be plugged in and unplugged easily for fender installation or removal.

When he had the bulbs and retaining rings installed, Grant moved on to the taillight. Before that could be installed on the left rear fender, it had to be installed onto the fender bracket and then the bracket installed onto the fender. Again Grant was careful to be sure of a good ground.

The to-do list was getting smaller, which made Grant happy, but the next item was to install the factory decals. He had done his research on where they went, and it took him less than five minutes to install all the decals except the Ford script on the front and rear fenders. What his papa had said kept coming back to him. "I would much rather have that script hand painted." Grant wasn't an artist, but if Papa wanted the script hand painted instead of decals, then hand painted it would be. Grant searched through the tool box and through all the drawers he could find in the garage and couldn't find any small, fine paint brushes. Then he thought of his grandmother and smiled.

He went into the house and down the hall to the small bedroom, his grandparents had referred to as the craft room. Back in time, the room had been his Aunt Wendy's bedroom. Then after she grew up and moved out, Grandma had started storing and doing her crafts in there. Grant could remember getting little gifts Grandma Jan had made. Not a holiday or birthday or any other notable event passed without getting something really clever and cute from Grandma Jan and it was always hand-made. As he looked around the room, he realized the room was untouched. Everything was where Grandma Jan had placed it. He suddenly had misgivings about disturbing anything, even for such a good cause. He even spotted an antique cut glass drinking glass with a fist-full of paint brushes of various sizes sitting on one of the shelves. He just couldn't bring himself to borrow one. If Papa hadn't touched anything in this room, then he wouldn't either. Grant slowly backed out of the room, turned the light out and closed the door. Walking back out of the house, Grant's mind was busy figuring out what to do next. He needed a fine tip paint brush. Then he smiled and pulled Papa's phone out of his pocket.

Stephanie had a whole packet of artist brushes. She had just bought them with the idea of trying her hand at painting. "Your grandfather suggested that I get out of the house more often." She said with a laugh as she handed the package to Grant. "Have you had anything to eat or drink?" Stephanie asked with the same concerned tone of voice that his mother always used. Grant figured it was something that just naturally occurred within the human female.

"I'm fine, really." Grant said. "I'll bring back what I don't use."

"No rush," Stephanie replied. "I haven't even bought any paints yet anyway."

"Well, thanks." Grant said as he turned away from her door and made his way back to the garage.

Grant mixed a small cup of red paint and tried three times to follow the raised script letters stamped into the sides of the front and rear fenders. He just couldn't seem to get a smooth line. He simply wasn't an artist. He felt his heart sink. He wanted the lettering to be hand painted but knew if he did it, the tractor would look better without it. He very carefully wiped the evidence of his efforts off the fender. If the script was going to get painted like Papa wanted it, he had to find another way.

Grant walked back over to the work bench trying to think of another way. He looked up and said a silent prayer. He wasn't asking for himself, but for his papa.

Grant had just turned his attention back to his notes on the workbench when he heard a car pull into the driveway. He felt a sick feeling that his mom or Jason had come to pick him up. He turned around ready to plead his case when he almost froze in place. It wasn't Jason or his mom. The visitors were getting out of their car and he couldn't believe what he was seeing. He stood motionless while his visitors walked into the garage through the open roll-up door.

"Grant?" Emily Roberts spoke first. She looked so different. Instead of the black plastic glasses held together with tape, she wore a cute pair of contemporary wire frames that made her eyes look bluer than ever.

"Emily? What are you doing here?" Grant's mind suddenly seemed to disconnect.

"You two know each other?" Jim Roberts, Emily's father asked.

"Dad, this is Grant Crawford." It wasn't so much what she said, as the way she said it, and the way her father reacted to it, "Grant, this is my Dad."

Grant stepped forward and reached around the tractor for Jim's hand. "Mr. Roberts."

"Grant, a pleasure to meet you." Mr. Roberts said with a big smile. "You two have done an amazing job on this old Jubilee. She looks better than she probably did when new."

"Thanks," Grant replied.

"Is your grandfather around?" Emily asked. The moment she asked the question, both she and her father noticed a change in Grant's demeanor. His shoulders sagged, his eyes dropped to the floor and he shook his head no. "Is everything all right?"

"Papa had a heart attack." Grant explained about the stints, and then the by-pass. He told them that his papa was in recovery and that the doctor had told his mom that everything had gone as well as could be expected.

"Is there anything we can do?" Emily asked.

"No, but thanks." Grant smiled at her.

"Well, we better be going then." Jim Roberts said. "I have to be at a client's in a few minutes."

Emily smiled at Grant. "Tell your grandfather that we are thinking of him and will pray for him." Then she turned to follow her dad out to their car.

Suddenly it hit Grant. "Emily, wait, please."

Emily and her dad both spun around on their heels and looked at him. "What?" Emily asked.

"You take art in school right?"

"Yes."

"You're good at it too, right?"

"Well, I don't know about that." Emily blushed a little, which made her so cute in Grant's eyes.

"Yes Grant, she is very gifted," Jim replied. "What did you have in mind?"

Grant was suddenly motioning with his hands for them to come back into the garage. "Please come and look at this." He took them to the painted fenders and explained that his papa had wanted the raised script letters to be painted instead of using the provided decals. He also explained that he was terrible at being an artist and almost ruined the fenders trying. "Is this something you could do?" Grant finally asked Emily directly.

Emily turned, and with her eyes, silently asked her father for permission to stay. Jim looked at his daughter, then at the boy that had stood up for her at the cost of getting himself expelled from school. He didn't really know this boy, but he knew the boy's grandfather. "You can stay." Jim finally said. "I will pick you up on the way back home. Shouldn't be more than an hour or two. Okay?"

"That should be fine, Dad. Thanks" Emily replied.

"Thank you, Mr. Roberts." Grant added.

Jim Roberts smiled and nodded to Grant. "Good luck, kids."

As soon as her father had left, Emily turned to face Grant. "Okay Mr. Crawford, you have an assistant. Do you have paint and a good brush?"

Grant felt like a fish out of water. Mr. Crawford?? Guess God does answers prayers. In spades!

Emily smiled a shy, faint smile, but a cute smile none-the-less. "Well?"

"Ah, yes, yes. I have some brushes right here, and I had mixed up some paint just before you got here." Grant quickly went to the work bench and retrieved the paint and brushes.

Emily had returned to the fenders and was looking them over when she noticed the brush that Grant had used in his failed effort. There was only the slightest speck of

185

red on the very tip of it. She picked it up and looked it over. "I'll use this one."

"It didn't work very well for me." Grant warned her.

"It might have if you had actually put some paint on it." Emily giggled.

Grant looked at her, and couldn't help but smile himself. "Okay, I admit it. I am not an artist."

"Oh?" Emily motioned to the painted fenders before her. "Did you paint these?"

"Well, yeah." Grant answered. "That's not being an artist, that's just being a painter."

"Oh?" Emily replied.

"You say that a lot, don't you?" Grant teased.

"My favorite response, actually." Emily laughed for the first time that Grant had ever seen. Her teeth had been fixed. He recalled that whenever she had smiled at school, she had always covered her mouth. It was wonderful to see her actually laugh without trying to hide her teeth.

Grant just crossed his arms and smiled.

"It allows people a chance to explain themselves, or defend their position without actually being confronted." Emily explained. "So you want to explain the difference between a painter and an artist?"

Grant suddenly realized that he was in over his head with this girl. She wasn't just smart, she was way smart. Too smart for the likes of him. "Nah, I think I'll just save myself time and embarrassment and plead the fifth."

186

Emily laughed out loud. There was something about this boy. Grant always managed to make her feel special. "We better get to painting before my dad gets back."

While Emily carefully traced the outer edge of the letters and then filled in the center, Grant watched. Her hands were so slender and soft, and they gently moved the brush in steady even strokes. In the time it took him to totally mess up one letter, she had painted the entire script on the first fender. As she started on the second fender, she glanced up at Grant watching her.

"Am I making you nervous?" Grant asked.

"Not at all," Emily answered with a smile and then turned the tables. "Am I making you nervous?"

Grant laughed thinking he was so out of his league. "Do I have to answer that?"

"No," Emily smiled while concentrating on her painting. "But may I ask you another question?"

"One I have to answer?"

"Not if you don't want to."

"Then I have nothing to lose, ask away." Grant replied.

"Why?" Emily asked.

"Why what?" Grant didn't get it.

"Why did you hit those boys?"

Grant didn't answer at first, what could he say that wouldn't make her think he was just as bad of a bully as

187

they were. "I didn't like what they were saying to you. I had warned them before to stop it."

Emily glanced up from her work but didn't say a word.

"You probably think I am just as bad as they are." Grant frowned.

"No. I don't." Emily stood up after finishing the second fender and looked Grant in the eyes for a moment before moving on to the first of the rear fenders. "I felt terrible that you got into trouble for it. I wish you hadn't done it."

"Have they bothered you since then?" Grant asked.

"Not at all."

"Then it was a win-win situation." Grant smiled.

"How is that?" Emily asked without taking her attention away from the lettering.

"I got the message through their thick heads, and got to spend two incredible weeks getting to know my grandfather." Grant replied. "I wouldn't have missed these past two weeks for anything."

Emily nodded her head in appreciation of that answer. As she stood up from finishing that fender and before moving on to the last one, she looked at Grant. "And what message did you get through those thick heads?"

"That there is a price to be paid for bullying pretty girls." Grant instantly replied without thinking first. Emily instantly blushed, which made Grant ashamed of his answer. "Oh, I am sorry. I didn't mean to offend you."

188

"You didn't offend me," Emily softly replied. "Just not used to being referred to as pretty."

"Well, you are." Grant said. "I also know how it feels to be made fun of."

Emily had already started lettering the last fender. She stopped and looked over at Grant. "Who has made fun of you?"

"A lot of people." Grant replied. "I hear their remarks. They think I don't, but I do."

"What do they say?" Emily had only heard what other girls had said about Grant, and most of that was how cute he was. Once in a while, someone would add that he wasn't very bright, but with looks like that, he didn't need to be.

"They call me stupid," Grant answered. "I'm not stupid. I just have a hard time keeping focused in class, and somehow missed things along the way and now find myself so far behind the class."

"Have you asked for help?"

"No." Grant quietly replied.

"Why haven't you?" Emily stopped what she was doing and looked into Grant's eyes.

"Because, that would be like admitting I'm stupid." Grant frowned. "I'm not stupid. I can learn things just as fast as anyone else. Look at what I've learned in just these last two weeks!"

"I never said you were stupid." Emily defended her position. "In fact, I never even thought it. I can see how

189

gifted you are, but you need to learn to ask for help when you need it."

Grant just shrugged, and Emily went back to lettering and in a couple of minutes finished the job. Grant was amazed at how perfect she had done it. "You are amazing." He said with a touch of awe in his voice.

"I did the easy part," Emily laughed. "Painting these fenders so they look brand new was the tough part, and you did that."

"That was nothing compared to the lettering." Grant insisted.

"Well, maybe God gives each of us certain talents so we can help each other," Emily smiled. "Now, what can I wash this brush out with?"

22

Grant got a small plastic cup with lacquer thinner in it and some paper towels for Emily to clean her brush. He watched as she thoroughly cleaned the paint out of it and then carefully dried it so the bristles were flat and straight. "How long should I wait before trying to mount those fenders?" He asked.

"So long as you don't stick your fingers in the wet paint, you could probably do it now," Emily replied with a smile. "If you like, I'll help you with that until my dad gets back."

"That would be great." Grant smiled. He really liked Emily. She wasn't the typical girlish girl. She was willing to step in and help get the job done. He led her over to the paint jig, and they carefully removed the front fenders and the nose centerpiece. Grant stepped over to the bench and retrieved the new medallion and installed it into the nose piece. Then with Emily holding the fenders, he bolted the nose piece to the fenders making the three pieces one. While he was bolting the pieces together, he mentioned that she hadn't really answered his question.

"What question?"

"What you are doing here?" Grant replied. "And why you were looking for Papa?"

"A week ago, your grandfather hired me to help him take care of the gardens," Emily answered. "And teach him how to care for them."

"But why you?" Grant asked.

"Why not me?" Emily looked at him with a fake hurt expression on her face. "He wanted the best."

Grant laughed. "Seriously, how did he find you?"

"Mrs. Jergens actually told me about the job. He had called her seeking someone to help him, and she referred me."

"Okay," Grant nodded that he understood that part. "But why did he call for help at our school and not the community college or a florist?"

"Well, a florist is good at arranging flowers, but maybe not the best at growing them," Emily replied. "I don't know why he called our school, maybe he just didn't think of the college." She paused a moment and then asked. "What are you driving at?"

"I don't know, actually," Grant admitted. "My papa is really smart. He asked me several times why I did what I did, and then he hires you. Coincidence?"

"Maybe you are reading too much into all of this," Emily answered. "He does need help learning how to care for the gardens, and calling the botany teacher at the school is a logical choice, but now that you mention it, there are a couple of other puzzling pieces to this puzzle."

"Oh?"

"That's my line." Emily laughed. "Two days after I took this job helping your grandfather, my dad got a call from a semi-retired dentist who just so happens to need some carpentry work done, and mentions that he heard I was good with plants and gardens."

"That could only have come from one place." Grant noted.

"You're right." Emily agreed.

"And let me guess, this dentist is Burt Herrington."

"Bingo!" Emily smiled. "When we get to his place, he and my dad go over what work he wants my dad to do, while Mrs. Herrington and I talk about building three flower gardens in their yard. During the conversation, she seems to suddenly notice my bad teeth and makes an offer to include dental work as part of my compensation."

"Still think it is a coincidence?" Grant asked.

"No. I think your grandfather set it up, to be honest." Emily agreed.

"The question is, how did he know about you?" Grant puzzled. "He asked me several times what happened at school, but I never wanted to talk about it, so he didn't get you out of our conversations."

"Then he must know someone at our school," Emily concluded. "Your grandfather is a clever and resourceful man." She thought Grant was a chip off the old block, but she didn't say it.

"Are you okay with that?" Grant asked.

"Okay with that? What do you mean?"

"Well, that he pried into your business." Grant answered.

Emily flashed the most beautiful smile, and Grant noticed something in her eyes, he didn't know what, but whatever it was, it made her whole face seem angelic. "I am more than okay with that. Grant, my daddy is a wonderful man. Loving, honest, hard-working, but poor. He gives us everything he can, but proper dental care was just beyond his reach. I knew how bad my teeth looked, and sometimes they hurt even worse than they looked. Every night I prayed to God for help. Help for my daddy to find enough work, and that somehow, someway, we could find a means to end the suffering and embarrassment my sister's and my teeth caused us. Your grandfather was the means by which God answered my prayers. Through your grandfather, my father has more work than he can handle right now, and because of him and Dr. Herrington, both my sister and I have teeth that we no longer have to suffer from or hide."

"You really believe in God?"

"Oh Grant, I do believe," Emily smiled so beautifully. "When we had lost everything and had to leave the farm, we had nothing but God. We didn't have a home, food, or more than a few changes of old clothes to wear. I remember the day we had to leave the farm. We stood at the end of the drive and my parents were crying. We joined hands and prayed as hard as we could for some form of salvation. While we were praying, an elderly couple who were driving down the road stopped next to us and asked if we needed help."

"Really?" Grant was enthralled with the story.

"Really," Emily replied. "It turned out that the couple had just purchased an old run-down house next to their own. The man offered it as a place for us to stay for free in exchange for my dad fixing it up. They also got their church to provide some old appliances and much-needed food to tide us over until Daddy could find work. When the

194

couple saw how good Daddy was at fixing things, they spread the word at church and others hired Daddy, which put food on the table but not much else. That was of course until your grandfather got involved. Now Daddy is getting calls almost every day."

"Wow." Was all Grant could think of saying. By this time, he had the front fenders and the nose piece bolted together. "Okay, I'll take this side and you that side." Grant explained what he wanted Emily to do to fit the front clip to the chassis. While he was bolting the fenders to the dash unit, Emily continued.

"The key to God's answer to my prayers was you."

"Me?" Grant stopped what he was doing and looked at her.

"If you hadn't done what you did, your grandfather wouldn't have gone looking into why you did what you did. Because you did what you did, and because he cared so much about you and tried to understand why you did it, he found me. Just how he found me, and who he knows at the school is beyond me, but it fits. God works in mysterious ways and whether you believe it or not, God used you to answer my prayers."

"If you say so." Grant wasn't fully convinced. The front clip was fully attached to the dash unit, so Grant moved to the front and loosely bolted the doglegs, which are panels that run from the fenders down the front edge of the tractor to the frame. He then installed the grille and tightened the dogleg bolts. The next piece to go on was the heavy steel grille guard that acted like a front bumper for the tractor. Emily helped hold it while Grant took the nuts off the front axle bolts that served to anchor the grille guard in place.

"You don't believe in God?" Emily asked while Grant worked.

"Sort of, I guess." Grant replied while not stopping what he was doing.

"Sort of? You guess?"

"Well, yeah." Grant replied.

"Grant, you either believe or you don't," Emily said. "It's like the weather, it is either raining or it's not."

"Like the weather," Grant countered. "You can have extremely high humidity and still not be raining. I want to believe, just not sure if I do. How can you be so sure? Look at everything you've lost."

"And look at everything he has replaced that with," Emily corrected. "Look at us. Where we are right now. If my family was still living on the farm, I would have still been going to my old school. Our paths would never have crossed. You wouldn't have done what you did, would never have gotten expelled, and you would never have gotten to spend this time with your grandfather. He would not have gotten involved in trying to understand why you did what you did, and he would never have gotten his friends to help my daddy and our family out."

Grant thought about that while he finished tightening the bolts to the grille guard. Then he reached under the hood and plugged the headlight wires into the one he had strung forward from the dash. Satisfied that the wires were safely out of the way of the fan, he went back to the dash and pulled the light switch.

"Wow! They work." Emily laughed. "Great job!"

"Just like they are supposed to do. Thanks." Grant winked at her. Then he stepped over to the work bench and grabbed an angle grinder and proceeded to grind a bare spot on the left rear axle housing, and a matching one on the bottom of the left rear fender.

"Why did you just grind that paint off?" Emily was surprised at what he had done.

Grant smiled at her. "Well, my pretty little lady friend, let me explain to you the importance of ground."

He proceeded to tell her what he had learned from Billy while she held the left rear fender in place, and he slid the big bolts through the holes in the axle housing and tightened them up. He then pulled the wires for the taillight together and tested it. It worked as advertised and made Emily cheer. The last piece to go on the tractor was the right rear fender, and when tightened in place, they stood back and admired the finished tractor.

"It is beautiful!" Emily said.

"Thanks, I couldn't agree more." Grant replied. "So you think God intended for us to meet?"

Emily turned and looked Grant in the eyes. "I do. For what purpose, I have no idea. Maybe for the blessings, we have already enjoyed and maybe for blessings yet to come."

"Such as?" Grant was more than just a little intrigued by that statement.

197

"I'm not sure," Emily admitted. "I have been richly blessed with answers to prayers that I have sought for some time. One such future blessing could be the opportunity to give back."

"What do you mean?"

"You said that you have fallen behind the class and didn't want to ask for help because that would be admitting you need help."

"Yeah, so?" Grant replied.

"Maybe I am supposed to be that help. Tutor you to get you back up to speed with the class. I could never have done what you did here with this tractor, but I can help you with school work."

Grant thought about that for a moment. "Miss Emily, you are very talented at a lot of different things. In fact, you remind me a lot of my late Grandmother Jan."

"Really? Tell me about her."

Grant spent ten minutes telling her all about his Grandma Jan, then he took her into the house and showed her around. Taking in all the little touches that exemplified who and what Grandma Jan was. When he showed her the craft room and explained how he couldn't bring himself to touch anything in it, mainly because Papa hadn't touched anything, it really touched Emily's heart. She told Grant that she now understood his grandfather's desire to save her gardens, and she also felt a special bond growing between her and Grant. They were sitting on lawn chairs in the garage talking when her father pulled into the drive.

Mr. Roberts was speechless as he walked around the finished tractor. When he finally did find his voice, he kept telling Grant what a wonderful job he had done and how proud he should be of it.

"It wouldn't look as great as it does if you hadn't allowed Emily to help." Grant replied. "Nor would it be done now. I really appreciate it. It made all the difference."

While they were talking and admiring the tractor, Stephanie came up the drive with a covered dish in one hand and a bottle of soda in the other. She couldn't believe that she was looking at the same tractor she had just seen a few hours ago. She kept saying how beautiful it was and how proud John was going to be. She was so taken with the tractor that she nearly forgot why she had come over.

"You have to be about half starved," Stephanie said as she handed the food and drink over to Grant.

"I'm fine, really." Grant felt odd at accepting the food in front of Emily and her dad.

"Now listen," Stephanie scolded him. "You have been here since early morning, and here it is late afternoon. I know you haven't had a thing to eat, and only that coffee you made to drink. You really have to eat."

"You better listen to her, young man." Jim Roberts warned. "Women don't like to make a meal for a man and have them not eat it."

"You've got that right." Emily chimed in, enjoying the embarrassed look on Grant's face.

While they were trying to get Grant to eat, a pickup pulled into the drive and parked right behind Jim's car. A moment later, Billy walked into the garage. Grant introduced him to everyone and watched as Billy slowly worked his way around the tractor, silently appraising what he saw. Occasionally, Billy would stoop down and look closely at one thing or another. Then, without asking permission, Billy wobbled the gear shift to be sure of neutral and then started the tractor. He looked at the gauges and nodded at what he saw. Next, he tried the lights and watched the amp gauge as he did so. When he finally turned the lights and then the engine off, he turned to Grant.

"Boy, you did awesome! I couldn't have done a nicer job of wiring this thing than you did."

"Thanks." Grant smiled at the praise.

"You wired it?" Jim Roberts was equally impressed. He had thought it was a purchased wiring harness.

"I did." Grant replied. "I couldn't have done it though without Billy's guidance. He spent time last night showing me how to do it, and drew up a diagram that was so easy to follow. He made it a job I could do."

"You're too modest boy," Billy laughed. "I just pointed you in the right direction, you did the work. And I have to say, it is beautiful work. The paint looks awesome as well. The hand painted script really sets it off."

"Don't touch it!" Grant barely got out before Billy's finger got into Emily's wet paint, which made everyone laugh. "Emily just painted those. Again, help from someone doing what I couldn't have done."

Billy smiled at Grant, "Miss Not Directly?" Grant's eyes went wide and he clenched his lips at Billy, which got the "hush" statement across, making Billy laugh and wink.

Stephanie, who was standing next to Emily and had also been wondering about her connection to Grant, thinking they made a cute couple, placed her arm around the petite girl. "You painted that lettering?"

Emily just nodded that she had.

"Oh my, what a talented duo you and Grant are!" Stephanie proclaimed, which really made Billy laugh but caused an awkward moment for the other three.

23

Debbie's motherly instinct to worry kicked in when she pulled up to her father's house and then had to park in the street because the drive was full. She was instantly worried that something bad had happened. She was out of her car and running up the drive the moment she shut the car off. As she approached the garage, she could see that nothing was amiss and that all these people seemed to be admiring the tractor. She paused in the drive and caught her breath and for the first time noticed that the tractor was back together and absolutely beautiful!

As she entered the garage, the sight of the tractor actually left her speechless for a few moments. When she did find her voice, tears were running down her cheeks as she praised Grant for what he had accomplished. Grant, who was by this time standing next to Emily, leaned down and whispered to her. "This is becoming embarrassing."

"Be gracious," Emily whispered back to him. "You've exceeded everyone's expectations."

"Well, I won't let that happen again." Grant whispered.

"Of course not," Emily arched up on her toes to whisper back. "From now on, people are going to expect great things from you." Grant looked down at her and frowned. Emily was smiling and winked at him. On the other side of the tractor, Jim Roberts noticed the whispered conversation and reactions between Grant and his daughter and had no doubt about the meaning of it all. What did surprise him, was his own reaction to it, a calm acceptance.

That was when Debbie took notice of the cute, petite girl standing next to her son and the looks they gave each other. Without a moment's hesitation, she turned and marched right up in front of the kids and introduced herself.

"Hi, I'm Grant's mother."

"Mom." Grant tried to calm his mother. He had seen her act like this before and it wasn't a good sign. It all made Emily smile. Somehow she saw the humor in it. With her angelic face, bright blue eyes, and that innocent smile, Debbie thought this girl was probably the cutest little girl she had ever seen, but there was something familiar about her.

"I'm Emily Roberts," Emily spoke up. "Grant and I go to the same school. The man on the other side of the tractor is my father." Debbie turned to see which man Emily was referring to and spotted Jim Roberts standing next to Billy and looking her way. The moment she saw Jim, Debbie remembered when she had seen Emily before. She was one of the girls that had bought a dress for a dollar and paid with quarters.

"How did you find out Grant was doing this tractor?" Debbie asked, afraid deep down that somehow Grant had let her down again. Emily was about to reply when her dad came around the tractor and introduced himself to Debbie. He explained how they had shown up to work in the gardens, and learned of her dad's heart attack. Since he had planned on leaving Emily here to help John with the gardens while he made another business call, and when Grant asked for her help, he didn't see any harm in letting her stay and help.

"I'm confused," Debbie admitted. "My dad hired you to help him with the gardens?"

Emily nodded yes.

203

Jim explained that John had called the school botany teacher looking for help and that teacher had recommended Emily for the job. He then turned to Emily and asked if she had taken care of the gardens yet?

"No Daddy, we just finished putting this back together when everyone showed up."

"Then you better go do that now, we have to be getting home soon."

Emily nodded and bowed her head slightly toward Debbie. "It is nice to meet you, Ma'am." Then she stepped past Grant and Debbie and walked out of the garage and around the corner toward the back yard and the gardens.

"Since she helped me with this," Grant said motioning toward the tractor. "I'll go help her with the gardens." Before Debbie or Jim could do or say anything, Grant was out the door and around the corner. Stephanie, who had been off to the side, but within earshot of the conversation, stepped in and explained that Grant needed Emily's talent as an artist to paint the script lettering on the fenders of the tractor. When she finished that, she helped Grant put all the metal pieces on the tractor to finish it up. "Quite a young lady you have there, Mr. Roberts."

Debbie turned around and looked at the script lettering. It looked as though it had been professionally done. "She is really good," Debbie admitted.

"Not just at lettering," Jim said. "Emily is a good girl, through and through."

Debbie looked at Jim for a moment. "I am so sorry if you thought I was implying anything else. It just came as a shock to me, that's all. Grant has never mentioned her at all, or any girl for that matter."

"I understand," Jim replied. "Emily has only mentioned Grant once when he stood up for her against those bullies."

It suddenly all fell into place for Debbie.

"That son of yours is quite a young man as well," Jim said.

"Yes, he is," Debbie sighed her agreement.

"And he is smart enough to know how to pick the right kind of girl," Stephanie added, which made both Jim and Debbie turn back to look at her. Stephanie looked at the two parents and their surprised expressions. "Well, for Heaven's sake you two, open your eyes!"

Debbie and Jim exchanged an unreadable look, and then Jim shrugged. Debbie slowly made her way to the corner of the garage, just far enough outside to gain a view of the gardens in the back yard. The kids had their backs to her. Grant was watering half of the first garden while Emily was dead-heading the flowers. She could see that they were talking about something, but was too far away to know what.

"I think our parents are reading more into this than they ought to be." Grant said.

"Well," Emily laughed. "We are not being marched back to our cars by an angry parent. That's a good sign."

Grant laughed at that. "Yeah, I guess you're right about that. Guess that means they are okay with it."

"Okay with what, exactly?" Emily asked in a serious tone, but there was a hint of a tease in it.

Grant blushed. "With whatever they think is between us."

"A tractor?" Emily noted sourly. "They are okay with us having a tractor?"

That made Grant laugh out loud. Loud enough for both Debbie and Jim, who was by now standing next to her at the corner of the garage, to hear.

"Well, all friendships have to start somewhere." Grant noted.

"And it is a pretty nice tractor." Emily agreed.

"I have an idea," Grant said. "What about the fall dance coming up?"

Emily stopped pulling dead blossoms off and stood up looking Grant in the eyes. "Are you asking me to the fall dance?"

"Well, yeah." Grant sheepishly replied. "Miss Emily Roberts, would you honor me by attending the fall dance with me?"

Emily looked at Grant for a moment without answering. Just long enough to cause concern in Grant's heart. "On one condition, Mr. Grant Crawford."

"Oh?"

"Don't go stealing my line, it won't help your cause."

"Okay, what is the condition?" Grant asked.

Emily placed her right hand on her hip and pointed the index finger of her left hand right at Grant. "The condition is that you put the same amount of effort into your school work as you put into that tractor in there, and bring your grades up high enough to pass."

Grant looked at her with a fallen expression. "That's completely different."

"Oh? How so?"

"I don't know where to begin," Grant defended his position. "I'm so far behind the class."

"If I had asked you two weeks ago to put that tractor together, could you have done it?"

"Two weeks ago? No, I couldn't have begun to put a tractor together then."

"What changed that?" Emily asked, guiding the conversation the direction she wanted it to go.

"I learned a lot from Papa, Billy, and, well you." Grant's voice trailed off as he noticed the "Gotcha" smile spreading across Emily's face as she planted her left hand on her hip to match the right. "You set me up, didn't you?"

This time, it was Emily that laughed out loud. Jim reached out and gently nudged Debbie back around the corner of the garage and out of sight of the kids.

"I don't know what kind of relationship exists between your son and my Emily," Jim admitted. "I do, however, know this. I know your father, and I admire the kind of man he is. Through Grant, I can see a lot of your father. Emily and her sister Amy mean the whole world to me, but because of things beyond my control, they haven't had a lot in life to laugh about. I couldn't afford to give them the things that other girls had. Never once did Emily ever complain. She just accepted life as it came, and lived her life to the best of her ability with grace and a strong sense of faith. She is such a good girl that I have always wondered why I was so blessed just to be her father. There hasn't been much in life to make her laugh, but Grant does. I appreciate that fact. I also appreciate that when other kids ridiculed her for her old clothes, bad teeth and taped glasses, your son had the character to see through all of that, to see Emily for the beautiful person she is. It is almost as if he could see her heart, and he stood up for her. Protected her from the pain of their ridicule. Sadly, it cost him dearly, and I am sorry for that."

By now Debbie was in tears. "I never knew why Grant had been expelled, other than that it was for fighting. He wouldn't explain his actions. Not why he had done it, or for whom. Now, I can see why. Thank you for telling me. This all has simply caught me off-guard. Grant really is a good kid."

"I'll say." Stephanie had walked over to where Jim and Debbie were talking when she noticed Debbie tearing up. She put her arm around Debbie's shoulders. "That boy saved his grandfather's life the other morning with his quick thinking and actions. This whole tractor business, working so hard these last couple of days, just to please his papa. That speaks volumes for that boy's character."

208

Debbie peeked around the corner of the garage at the kids. They were both working in the second garden by then and talking very animatedly. When Debbie pulled back around the corner, she commented. "I wish I knew what they are talking about."

Stephanie leaned in and kissed Debbie's cheek. "Be very careful what you wish for." Then Stephanie turned on her heels and walked down the driveway toward her home.

Jim looked down at his watch, just as Billy walked past them and told Debbie to tell the boy what a great job he had done. "Oh dear," Jim said. "I better get Emily home. Her mother probably already has supper on the table." He stepped around the corner and called out. "Emily, are you about ready to go home?"

"Yes, Daddy. Be right there." Emily replied and then turned to Grant. "Would you mind, taking care of the waterhose for me?"

"Sure thing," Grant said with a smirk, just seconds before he lightly sprinkled her with the cold water.

"Grant Crawford!" Emily squealed. "Now I have to ride home in my daddy's car all wet!"

"You're not all wet." Grant replied with a smile as he reached down with his right hand and plucked a rose from a bush and offered it to Emily. "Forgive me?"

Emily couldn't help but smile as she reached out for the offered rose and noticed the two spots of fresh blood on Grant's right hand. "It poked you, didn't it?"

"I had it coming." Grant replied with that smile of his that she found so enchanting.

"You shouldn't plunder your grandmother's roses."

"Not to worry," Grant replied. "If anyone would understand, it would be her."

Debbie and Jim smiled at each other, the symbolism in Grant giving Emily a rose wasn't missed by Debbie.

24

Debbie watched Emily say goodbye to Grant, then turn away and walk to where she and Jim were standing. "Thanks for helping Grant today," Debbie said with a smile.

"It was my pleasure Ma'am, and very nice to meet you as well."

"Thank you honey, you too."

As the Roberts got into their car, Debbie turned and watched Grant coiling the hose up for a moment before turning around and looking at the tractor again. It truly was beautiful. She never thought she would think of a tractor as being beautiful, but it was. She slowly walked around it, noticing every little detail. Her dad had said that he didn't know if Grant would be a different boy by the time he went back to school. She had to smile as a tear rolled down her cheek. He was a different boy already, actually a different young man. He had taken on the task of finishing this project by himself. More important than that, was the attitude he adapted to do it. Failure was not an option. That thought made her smile, it was one of her father's favorite sayings. In just two short weeks, her son had become more like her father than anyone would have thought humanly possible. "Oh Daddy, you are not going to believe the difference you made in my son's life!"

When Grant came into the garage, his mother was standing next to the tractor with her back to him. She was sliding her right hand across the glossy finished hood. "Mom?"

Debbie spun around with tears rolling down her cheeks.

"You okay Mom?" Grant was concerned to see her tears.

"More than okay," Debbie walked over to him and wrapped her arms around him. "I have never had a prouder moment in my entire life. Deep down I always knew you had it within you to become what you have become in the last two days. An incredibly bright and talented young man. Standing here looking at this tractor just drove that home to me. You said you were going to do it, and not only did you do it, but you did such an incredible job of it."

"I had help, Mom." Grant was almost defensive. "Papa had gotten it to the point that allowed me to finish. Then Billy guiding me through the wiring, and Emily doing the lettering makes it all look as good as it does. I couldn't have done it without them."

"Life is about knowing when to ask for help," Debbie said.

Grant looked at his mother. "Yes, Emily! I got that point."

"What?" Debbie didn't get it.

"That is exactly what Emily just told me." Grant replied. "I asked her to the fall dance, she said yes on one condition."

"And that condition is?"

"That I get my grades up to a passing level before then." Grant frowned.

"Oh, I do like that girl."

"Oh yeah?" Grant smirked at his mother. "Well, me too."

"Okay," Debbie smiled and waved her hand toward the tractor. "You put together a successful plan to achieve this, what's the plan to win the date to the fall dance?"

"Simple," Grant laughed. "Have Emily help me achieve it. That way if I try really hard and still come up short, she might take pity on me and give me another chance."

Debbie laughed. "Not the plan I was hoping for, but I like the fact that you are getting good at formulating plans for success."

"I was more confident about finishing this tractor than I am about having a date for the dance."

Grant's first day back at school started with a five-minute warning speech in the principal's office. Grant assured him that he had no intentions of repeating his previous mistakes. Unfortunately, he didn't seem to have any luck in being in the halls at the right time to run into Emily. He was hoping for better luck at lunch. He had four classes in the morning and three more plus a one-period study hall, in the afternoon. The only class he shared with Emily was science at the very end of the day.

Grant had spent the weekend at his father's apartment. He had always enjoyed his time there as his father's greatest ambition in life was to play video games and drink beer. Grant had always enjoyed playing video

213

games with his dad, and for many weekends that was all they did. That weekend it all changed. Grant knew that he had to find a way to better his position. He thought of his papa's story about when he realized that he wanted to get to know Grandma. He came up with a plan and put that plan into action. The secret to Papa's success, Grant had concluded, was tenacity. If he had given the cause up as lost before he had run out of flowers, well, life as everyone in the family knew it, would have been different.

Grant's plan started with his own to-do list that he planned on making up every day. At the start of each class, Grant handed the teacher a letter inside an unsealed envelope. Each envelope had the teacher's name only on the outside. Some teachers opened the letter and read it before starting the class, others waited until the end of class, but in every case, the teachers responded in a positive way. The letter was simple and straightforward. In it, Grant admitted to failing to be involved in his school work. He promised change and asked for help. He explained how his past bad habits had left him in a position of feeling lost. He asked for reading material, and extra study work that the teacher might feel would help his cause.

At lunch, he sat off to the back of the cafeteria by himself. He had barely sat down and started reading a book about American History that one of the teachers had given him when he sensed someone approach. He looked up. It was Emily in a light blue dress that he remembered Grandma Jan wearing, and her sister Amy. Grant stood up so quick he hit the edge of the table with his long legs, which made both girls giggle. Grant blushed and apologized for his clumsiness.

"Don't apologize," Emily smiled. "I'm touched that you honored us by trying to stand. You okay?"

"Yeah, I'm fine," Grant replied and offered them a seat with a casual hand gesture.

"How is your first day back going?" Emily asked.

"As good as can be expected." Grant replied.

"What are you reading?"

"Just a book my history teacher thought might help me in her class."

"Oh?" Emily replied, which just caused Grant to look at her with a half smirk.

"Have a long uphill fight ahead of me," Grant admitted.

"I have faith in you," Emily said. "I also asked my parents if you could study with us. Daddy said you are welcome to come over after school two nights a week for now."

"Tell him I really appreciate it, and I do." Grant replied. "I plan on going to that dance."

Both Emily and Amy smiled, but only Emily spoke. "As do I."

At the end of the day, Grant chatted a few minutes with Emily, then packed all the books he was taking home into his backpack and left the school. His plan was to make a stop on his way home, but the books were so heavy, he stopped by the house and dumped the books off before heading to the hospital.

Grant spent an hour with his grandfather, and they talked mainly about what John had just been through. Not once did the tractor come up. Grant found that odd because it was the really big thing they shared. John did ask Grant to stop by the house tomorrow night and water the flowers if he wasn't out of the hospital by then.

That night over supper, Grant asked his mother if Papa had said anything to her about the tractor. He hadn't, and that really puzzled Grant and he could think of only two reasons. The first was, in his medical condition, Papa might have short term memory loss, or that it was just something for them to do while he was expelled and didn't mean as much to him as it did Grant. The second thought and the one Grant suspected to be the truth. Papa somehow knew what he had done, and wasn't going to spoil the surprise by discussing it before he went home and saw it for himself.

After supper, Grant went right to his room and hit the books. Debbie and Jason both noticed that Grant's television wasn't turned on, nor was he playing a video game. Two hours went by before Debbie checked in on him and found Grant hard at work. She smiled at him, he frowned back.

John didn't get released from the hospital the next day, and at lunch, Grant told Emily that he had to tend the gardens after school. She said her daddy had asked about the gardens and wondered if anyone was taking care of them. Since the gardens meant so much to John, her daddy had suggested that when the kids got home from school, he would run them over there.

216

"So he is okay with me coming home with you?" Grant asked, a bit nervous about it.

"Yes, he is," Emily replied with a straight face. "But you will have to be on your best behavior."

That comment made Amy laugh, and did nothing to ease Grant's nerves.

When they arrived at the Roberts' home after school, Jim took the whole family over to John's place to take care of the gardens. While the kids worked the gardens, Jim showed his wife the tractor. She was utterly amazed at how beautiful it was. When the gardens were taken care of, they returned home and the kids started on their homework. It didn't take long before everyone realized just how far behind his studies Grant truly was. Emily kept stopping her work to help Grant until he finally suggested that she let him flounder until she had her work completed.

When Emily couldn't seem to do that, Grant asked if he could move from the living room, where they were working, out to the kitchen table. At first, Emily protested, but Grant insisted that it was the only way. "The last thing I want to see," Grant explained. "Is your helping me hurt your own grades.

Amazingly, both Mr. and Mrs. Roberts got involved in helping Grant. Jim was more on Grant's level with school work and could easily understand the boy's frustration. It was clear where the Roberts' girls got their gift for understanding school work, Mrs. Roberts. When Jim and Grant got stuck on something, she stepped in and guided Grant through it. In less than an hour, Emily finished her work and took over tutoring Grant. They had just finished when Debbie knocked on the door to pick Grant up. When Grant closed the last book, he smiled at Emily.

"I can't thank you enough."

"You're very welcome." Emily reached out and patted his hand. "I enjoy being in your company."

"Me too." Grant smiled.

"You enjoy being in your company?" Emily barely got out before busting out laughing, which made Grant blush. This girl really is too smart for me, Grant thought.

"All finished with your homework?" Debbie asked as she was lead into the kitchen.

"Yes I am," Grant proudly announced. "For the first time in my life, I have done all of my homework!" This drew surprised expressions from everyone.

"You've never finished your homework before?" Amy asked. It was the first time she had ever spoken to Grant directly. She usually just listened and offered the occasional smile.

"No, never." Grant replied.

"How did you ever make it this far?" Emily was stunned.

"Charm." Grant smiled and gave her a wink, which made the Roberts laugh. Debbie just shook her head and said it was time to get that boy home, he was delusional. Before leaving, Grant thanked each of the Roberts family for their help and promised Emily that he wouldn't let her down.

After supper that night, Grant went into his room to pick up where he had left off on the history book the teacher had given him. The one thing he had learned that day was just how much he had to learn. The following day at school, he actually had completed assignments to turn in. Every one of his teachers took note of this. He also participated in classroom discussions, because for the first time in his life, he had a clue what they were talking about.

The next day, Grant had once again completed assignments to turn in, but it was clear that he had done them on his own. He also had a little more trouble participating in class because he was less sure of himself. The positive side of that was that he was honest with his teachers and explained his tutoring schedule. When they compared the work he did with Emily's help and the work he completed by himself, it gave the teachers a clearer picture of just where Grant stood on his learning curve and they could offer help and assign extra credit work to help him along.

At the end of the third period that Friday, he was called to the office. As he neared the glassed-in office, he noticed his mother waiting for him and he felt the pain of panic sweep through him. He burst through the door with tears already forming in his eyes.

"Is Papa okay?"

Debbie smiled. "He is just fine. I took him home this morning and got him settled. He asked if I could drop you off. The Principal said that you have been doing so well, that he didn't have a problem with you going home early today."

Grant gave his mother a big hug and then turned to the office secretary and asked that she pass a note to Emily Roberts that he had left.

25

When Debbie and Grant pulled into John's driveway, he was sitting on a lawn chair in the garage with the big roll-up door open. He smiled and waved at Debbie, she waved back and blew a kiss to him.

"You're not staying?" Grant asked.

"No, this is your time with Papa." His mother replied with a smile. "I'm heading back to work. I'll see you when I get off."

"Okay Mom," Grant leaned over and kissed her cheek and then got out of the car. As he walked toward the garage, John got up out of his chair slowly.

"Just sit and take it easy, Papa." Grant scolded him.

John flashed a big smile. "At my age son, I'll do as I want. Come here." John opened his arms and took Grant in them and hugged the boy as tight as he could without too much pain. When he released Grant, the two of them turned and looked at the finished tractor before them.

"I knew what you were doing," John said.

"I knew that you knew." Grant smiled. "That day in the hospital when we held hands. I saw it in your eyes."

John laughed. "Yes, I suppose you did. It was the look in your eyes that told me the same thing. I knew you were going to do this by yourself. I just never expected it to turn out so perfect. I can't tell you how proud I am of you."

"I had help, Papa," Grant admitted. "I needed it too. Billy, a friend of Jason's, helped by teaching me how to do the wiring. He even drew a diagram of the wiring that was easy enough for even me to follow."

"But you did the actual wiring." John countered.

"I did." Grant replied.

"And you painted the sheet metal by yourself."

"But you had taught me how to paint when we did the chassis." Grant pointed out.

"A chassis is easy to paint," John argued. "Sheet metal is far more delicate. One slip and it shows every sin."

"Well, I kept hearing you in my head telling me to keep the gun moving." Grant smiled.

John laughed at that. "And this lettering is factory sharp. I didn't teach you that."

"That's why I couldn't do it," Grant replied. "Your gardener, Emily Roberts, did the lettering and then helped hang the sheet metal on the tractor."

"Did she now?" John nodded his head with appreciation. "That young lady is quite something."

"Yes, she is." Grant agreed, silently debating about asking Papa to come clean on the whole deal, but just couldn't quite do it.

"Sit down Grant, please," John said as he pulled the second chair he had gotten out closer to his. "I hear great things about you. Your mother was going on and on about the change she has seen in you."

Grant just smiled.

222

"I want to thank you for the two weeks we had together," John said. "I feel so blessed to have been able to spend that time getting to know what a great young man you are."

"It is me that needs to thank you, Papa." Grant replied. "I knew you, but didn't really. I wouldn't have missed our time together for anything. I appreciate all the trouble you went through to occupy my time and to give me a sense of purpose. I guess even more important than any of that was when you charged me with building that jig. For the first time in my life, someone expected something of me and believed in me."

"You didn't let me down either." John nodded at the now empty jig. "Best painting jig I ever saw."

Papa," Grant looked his grandfather in the eyes. "I do have a question for you."

"Oh? John asked. Grant just smiled at that, but let it go.

"How did you find out about Emily?"

"Let's just say that sometimes God puts things into motion and leads us into a situation. If we are faithful and follow his lead, good things happen. Never pass up an opportunity to help someone. It is even better if you can do it unnoticed. When you stepped in and helped Emily and refused to take credit or gloat about it, I knew you had the right heart within you."

"Papa, how can you be so sure of God? And, given that if he does exist, that he set that whole thing in motion?" Grant asked.

223

John looked at his grandson a moment. "Grant, where would you be today if those boys hadn't taunted Emily?"

"I'd be right here talking to you, just as I am right now."

John smiled. "No, you wouldn't be, because I would be dead. You wouldn't have been here to save me. That tractor would still be sitting back there in that corner rotting away. Mr. Roberts would be searching for meaningful employment. Emily and her sister would still be suffering from their poor teeth. You would still be going through the motions without any direction or purpose in life. At the end of this school year you would fail your studies and be forced to repeat the year, and probably drop out of school next year when you turn sixteen."

Grant didn't respond, so John continued. "Because you made a stand for what was right, those boys learned that they can't go around hurting people. I feel so blessed that I got to know you, the real you. The you that no one even knew existed, including yourself. On top of that, I got to enjoy the best two weeks I can remember, doing something I have wanted to do for a very long time, save my dad's tractor. Jim Roberts found the work he needed, and my friends found an honest man to do the things they wanted to be done. Emily and her sister received the much needed dental work they so desperately needed to end their pain and suffering. Burt told me that those teeth had to have caused horrible pain for both girls. Not to mention the boost to their self-esteem. And just as important as all of that, your mother got the son she had always prayed for."

Grant didn't reply. He just sat there thinking about what Papa was telling him.

"Just remember Son, doing a good deed is like tossing a pebble into a pond. It isn't just the impact site that is affected. The ripples from that deed fan out touching the entire pond from shore to shore." *Amen*

"I didn't do it to create waves," Grant admitted. "I just wanted it to stop. Knocking them down was a spur of the moment thing, done without thought. Every time I saw it happening, I could see her pain, her anguish and shame. I could feel it inside me. They had no right. If all you say is true, did God make those boys so mean?"

John thought a moment. "Only God knows the purpose of His ways, but it is possible."

"How could He do that?" Grant wanted to know. "Of all people, Emily Roberts is probably the sweetest, kindest person I've ever met. She didn't deserve that pain and torment."

John smiled and reached out and placed his hand on top of Grant's. "It's very simple Son. She had to suffer to spark you into action. Because when you stepped in and rescued her, her life and many others have been blessed. It is on a very small scale the same as our relationship to God. Jesus didn't deserve to suffer either, but He did, and did so gladly to rescue us. To offer us a better life of peace and hope. Just as Emily is now free of the torment she suffered at the hands of those boys because of you. We too, are free of the bondage our sins placed us in because Jesus took those sins upon Himself." *Amen*

Grant didn't reply. He had never had a discussion about faith like this before. He could see the passion in Papa's eyes.

225

"Just as Emily hid her smile from the world because of her teeth, man hid from God because of our sins. God hates all sin and couldn't bear to look upon us draped in the filth of sin. Just as your mother loved you even when you least deserved it, God still loved us. Because of that undying love, He sent Jesus to wash those sins from us so God could once again look down upon His children."

Grant shrugged. "Emily believes as you do. I wish I had such faith. Such complete and unfaltering faith. To believe without doubts."

"There will always be doubt," John replied. "If not in God, then in God's plan for us. Just remember, that which can be proven beyond doubt is fact. That which is believed and yet unproven is faith. Jesus told His disciples, "Because you have seen me, you believe. Blessed are those who have not seen and yet believe." John paused a moment and then continued. "I believe in part because my parents believed, and their parents before them. It was how I grew up. Faith seemed stronger in the community back then. Like you, when I grew into a man, I too had my doubts. I turned to the Bible, and in it, I could find no fault. The one thing that truly struck a chord with me happened after the resurrection of Jesus."

"What was that?" Grant asked.

"All of the people that saw Jesus after the resurrection and spent time with Him before the ascension were changed people. Many of those died horrible and gruesome deaths that they could have avoided by simply denouncing that Jesus was the Christ, the son of the living God. They chose death realizing that the one real truth is everlasting and death is but a moment in time."

226

Grant nodded, a part of it was getting through and starting to make sense.

"I can only tell you what I believe and why," John said. "If I could give you faith, I would in an instant. If God offered to exchange my life for your faith, I would do it instantly. Because I love you that much. All I can do is ask that you seek Jesus, pray for Him to fill your heart. All you will ever need in life, He will provide. As Jesus himself promised, seek and yea shall find."

"I will Papa, I promise." Grant gripped John's hand and gently squeezed it.

They sat silently for a few moments, just happy to be in each other's company. Until a smile crossed John's lips. "Why did you decide to not use Grandma's paint brushes on the lettering?"

The surprise of being found out was all over Grant's face. "How did you know that?"

"Tracks Son. Tracks." John laughed. "You didn't take your shoes off when you went in the house. The tracks lead right into the craft room and stopped just inside the door. Then I noticed the package of brushes on the workbench. How did you come by them?"

Grant smiled and shook his head. He should have seen that coming, his mother always had a knack for knowing what he had done, and here was his mother with years more experience. "When I needed to paint the lettering, I searched in here for brushes but couldn't find any. That's when I thought about Grandma Jan, she always had tons of brushes for her projects. When I got in there, I saw that everything was as she had left it. If you couldn't touch any of it, then I couldn't either. I borrowed the brushes from Stephanie."

John looked at Grant with a sad smile. "You know Grant, maybe soon we can take all of these external memories of your beautiful grandmother and tuck them within us, where they belong."

26

From the time Grant had asked Emily for a date to the fall dance, he had six weeks to raise his grades. Also during this time, he had taken to staying most of the time with Papa to help him during his recovery. Somewhere along the line, John had almost fully recovered but Grant stayed on. On weekends that he wasn't obligated to spend with his father, Grant helped Papa launch the boat and they spent a lot of time on the river. Every time they took the boat out, they had guests. Sometimes it was Stephanie, sometimes it was Jason, Debbie, and little J.J.. Once it was the entire Roberts family, but always it included Emily and Amy. The two girls absolutely loved fishing and spending time on the river.

Both girls were natural fishermen. They could cast better than John or Grant and always caught the most fish. While they held their poles waiting for a bite, Emily would quiz Grant on some subject. At one point he asked what she wanted to be when she finished school.

"A teacher, of course," Emily replied.

"I think we better call the whole thing off right now then," Grant said.

"What?!" Emily demanded of him.

"I don't think I can spend the rest of my life taking these quizzes." Grant answered, which made Amy laugh so hard she almost fell into the water.

"I'm just making sure I have a date for the fall dance." Emily defended herself. "It might be hard to find a replacement at this late date.

Grant did bring his grades up, not just to a passing mark but high enough to give him a little bit of breathing room. It was funny when he thought about it, not only had his grades come up, but school work, in general, was easier for him. On the last school day before the dance, Grant asked each of his morning class teachers for a note stating that his grades were above the pass mark. It must have been the topic of discussion at lunch in the teacher's lounge because all of his afternoon teachers provided the note without him asking for it.

After school, Grant and Emily walked to Papa's place together. He had presented his documents of proof, as he called them, and she had confirmed that she planned on keeping her end of the bargain. They were excited about the big event. They would be going somewhere sort-of official as a couple, and they liked that idea. Emily said that her daddy had even offered to buy her a new dress for the occasion, but since he didn't have enough money to buy one for Amy as well, she had opted to just wear one of the nicer dresses that had been Grandma Jan's.

When they turned up the driveway, they were surprised to see that John had gotten Grandma Jan's car out and was washing it. The vacuum was out next to the car along with window cleaner and car wax.

"Papa, what are you doing?" Grant wanted to know. "You shouldn't be doing this."

"Nonsense," John replied. "It's high time I wash the dust off of this car. Besides, I want it to sparkle for the special occasion."

"What special occasion?" Emily asked.

"Why the big night," John smiled. "Grant, you did make the cut, didn't you?"

"Have the proof right here." Emily laughed waving all the signed teacher notes so John could see them.

"Well, in celebration, I am going to be your chauffeur tomorrow night." John laughed. "I promise you a wonderful night starting off with photo sessions with both sets of parents and then a fine meal at a special restaurant, and then off to the dance."

Emily and Grant looked at each other with raised eyebrows.

"Oh, and that reminds me of something. Emily, would you help me with something in the house?"

"Sure." Emily nodded.

"Grant please finish drying the car off so we can wax it as soon as I come back."

"Okay." Grant shrugged and reached down for a couple of dry towels and went to work.

While Grant started drying the car, John motioned for Emily to follow him. He led her down the hall to Jan's craft room. Once he turned the light on, John slid the closet door open and reached in and pulled a breathtaking teal satin dress out of the closet. The dress had a fresh dry-cleaning tag attached to the plastic bag that covered it. And a pair of teal colored pumps in an attached plastic bag. "I had coffee with your dad today." John looked Emily in the eyes. "Little girl, I have only ever met one woman of such deep compassion as you possess. Seeing how you turned down that new dress, I was hoping you would honor me and wear this one, if it isn't too old fashioned."

Emily broke into tears. "It is beautiful."

"My Jan wore this for our 25th anniversary," John explained. "It was the only time she ever wore it. When I asked her why, she said that she was saving it for a very special occasion. Since you are her size, I honestly can't think of an occasion more special than this."

"I can't," Emily choked out between sobs. "You have done so much for me already."

"Little lady, I would have given the world to be able to reach my grandson and help him to turn his life around. I realize it all happened because of you. If fate has this be the only date the two of you have, I want it to be as special as it can be. Although, I admit to hoping this is the beginning of something like Jan and I had, but that's up to God and the two of you. Besides, it would do my heart good to see a beautiful woman wearing this dress again, and I know that would also please Jan."

The night of the dance was as John had forecasted. He picked Grant up first at his mother's. He couldn't help but feel sorry for the boy, his mother was spit polishing him all the way out to the car. It was no different at the Roberts'. Mrs. Roberts had done Emily's hair in long curls with satin ribbons to match the dress and shoes. The shoes did require a bit of tissue shoved into the toes, but Emily

232

was beyond stunning in the dress. She might have been even prettier in it than Jan had been. A round of pictures were taken, half of which with Mrs. Roberts crying.

When they got to Debbie's, she burst into tears when she saw that dress on Emily. Wendy had grabbed it for the garage sale, but her dad had taken it off the sale rack and carried it back into the house without explanation. Seeing Emily in that dress looking like the most beautiful girl she had ever seen, filled Debbie with so much emotion she couldn't keep it in. She knew in her heart that she was looking at her future daughter-in-law.

When school ended for the year, Grant had managed to climb to somewhere in the middle of the class ranking. That summer Jim needed help in his booming carpentry business, and Grant went to work for him and the two got along as if they had been doing so all their lives. Emily never intended for it to happen, but as word got out about her gift with flowers, she found herself in a growing landscaping business. Instead of having date nights, Grant found himself working for Jim by day and Emily at night.

When they graduated from High School, Grant hadn't climbed any higher than the middle of the pack in class ranking, but Emily graduated class Valedictorian. In her speech, she honored a man that although a stranger at the time, and suffering through a great personal loss himself, had reached out to others. Because of this act of kindness, many lives have been forever changed. This is what she challenged her classmates to do. She noted that she was before them now because of her grades. She then reminded them that the only grade that matters in the end, would be the one received when we stand before God Almighty. *Amen*

Although Emily had hoped to go to college, under the pressure of her growing business, the Community College was the best she could handle, and then only a few courses at a time. In August of the following year, Grant and Emily were on an emergency call at her biggest commercial client. Somehow the sprinkler system had been damaged and when the timer set it off, it managed to send a sprout of water crashing down on a restaurant next door. The problem was that the client had forgotten to make the call until late in the afternoon.

So it was that on the hottest day of that year, Emily and Grant were struggling to dig up the broken lines and fix them before the automatic timer set water rushing through the system. Both were drenched in sweat and plastered in grass and dirt that was sticking to their skin. They had almost made it too, five more minutes would have made all the difference. Emily had wanted Grant to shut the main water supply off when they started the work, but he convinced her that to do that he would have to break the seal on the valve. Since she hadn't put any in the service truck, they didn't have a replacement. But if they worked fast, they could repair the damaged lines and not have to bother with getting a new seal from the office.

They had found the break in the lines, and dug back far enough to replace all the affected lines. They even got all the new lines glued into place and were about to install the new pop-up sprinkler head when Emily suddenly felt a rush of air.

234

"Oh no!" Was all she had gotten out when a jet of ice cold water under enough pressure to create a twenty-foot fountain, once it pushed her out of its way, blasted directly in her face. Not being one to give up, Grant grabbed the sprinkler head out of a stunned Emily's hand. Drowning in a gush of water that stung when it hit his face, Grant spent the next minute and a half forcing the sprinkler head against the water pressure until he finally got it to thread into the pipe. Of course, the head instantly popped up and continued drenching him in ice cold water until he had it secured.

The two dragged themselves out of the torrent of water and laid in the muddy grass catching their breath.

"We did it!" Grant finally proclaimed.

"We did it?" Emily sat up on one arm and looked at him like he was crazy. "Look at us."

Grant didn't bother getting up off his back. "You're beautiful."

"I look like a drowned rat!"

"Still beautiful."

Emily shook her head. "Grant Crawford! You're hopeless." By now Emily was kneeling in the wet grass watching all the sprinkler heads delivering water where they should. She finally struggled to her feet, entirely covered with a mixture of mud and grass. She looked down at Grant and offered a hand to pull him to his feet. "We better get these trenches filled back in," Emily noted, as Grant took her hand and pulled himself up, but not to his feet. He stopped at his knees and fished in his pocket for something, Emily didn't know what. Finally, a little plastic bag came out of his jeans pocket. Emily spotted the contents through the clear plastic instantly.

"Oh, my dear Lord." Emily gasped as she spotted the small gold band with the single diamond center. She put a filthy hand to her mouth and tears instantly began to roll down her cheeks. Not that anyone would have noticed, as wet as she already was.

"Emily Roberts," Grant began as he reached up and took her hand in his. "I think I fell in love with you the first moment I saw you, just as my Grandpa John fell for Grandma Jan. This was her ring, and I would like you to wear it as my wife for the rest of our days."

Emily dropped to her knees so hard into the muddy ground that it splattered up into Grant's face. She wrapped her arms around his neck and cried into his ear. "Yes, yes and yes!"

Made in the USA
Charleston, SC
02 September 2016